NEW

Step in

ANGLAIS

3e

WORKBOOK

Marie-Aude Ligozat
Direction pédagogique

Odile Bontout
Collège du Pont du Bois, Saint-Chéron

Danièle Broussaud
Collège Joseph Bara, Palaiseau

Aliki Diaz-Kostakis
École Polytechnique, Palaiseau

Maryse Pelletier
Collège Martin Luther King, Buc

PAPIER RECYCLÉ

Hatier

PLEASED TO MEET YOU ! ► pages 10 et 11

1. Repérage des formes verbales.

■ **Repère dans les pages 10 et 11 de ton manuel les verbes conjugués au présent simple, au prétérit et au *present perfect*, puis remplis le tableau suivant.**

présent simple	prétérit	*present perfect*
....	....	....
....	....	....
....	....	....
....	....	....
....		
....		
....		
....		
....		
....		
....		
....		
....		
....		

2. Les prépositions.

■ **Complète les phrases avec la préposition qui convient suivie d'un nom.**

1. I'm not very good ....

2. I get .... well with ....

3. I went .... two years ago.

4. I go .... school ....

5. I stayed ....

© HATIER PARIS 2003 – ISBN 978-2-218-74147-0

3. Like.

■ Complète les phrases avec un exemple personnel.

1. I look like .... but I don't look like ....
2. I like .... but I don't really like ....
3. I'd like to .... but I wouldn't like ....

4. Entraîne-toi à poser des questions.

■ Complète les questions suivantes.

1. I look like [**my mother**].
↓
.... you .... ?

2. I go to school [**by bus**].
↓
.... you .... to school?

3. I practise [**basketball**].
↓
.... sport .... you .... ?

4. The nicest person I know is [**my grandpa**].
↓
.... the nicest person you know?

5. I spent my holidays [**with my best friend**].
↓
.... you .... your holidays with?

6. I went to the Alps [**in August**].
↓
.... you .... to the Alps?

7. Yes, **I get up** early.
↓
.... you .... early?

8. No, **I won't look** for a job as soon as I leave school.
↓
.... you .... for a job as soon as you leave school?

9. No, **I've** never **been** to a concert.
↓
.... you ever .... to a concert?

10. Yes; **we went** to Morocco.
↓
.... you .... abroad?

QUIZ

► page 13

How much do you know about music?

1 **Put these different types of music in chronological order (number them from 1 to 6):**

... rhythm'n'blues

... jazz

... work songs

... rock

... rock'n'roll

... blues

2 **Black slaves were:**

allowed to sing in English ☐

not allowed to sing in English ☐

allowed to play the drums ☐

not allowed to play the drums ☐

3 **Which types of songs are based on the Bible?**

Negro spirituals and gospel ☐

the blues ☐

4 **The blues expresses:**

happiness ☐

sadness ☐

5 **The blues was born:**

at the times of slavery ☐

after the abolition of slavery ☐

6 **The first jazz bands appeared in:**

the South of the United States ☐

the West of the United States ☐

7 **Match the musician and the instrument.**

Charlie Parker •	• the piano
Louis Armstrong •	• the saxophone
Duke Ellington •	• the trumpet

8 **Rock'n'roll was born:**

in the early 1900s ☐

in the fifties ☐

in the sixties ☐

9 **Who was called "the King" of rock'n'roll:**

Mick Jagger ☐

Elton John ☐

Elvis Presley ☐

10 **Listen and number from 1 to 6 the instruments you are going to hear.**

... a trumpet

... a banjo

... a guitar

... a saxophone

... a drum

... a washboard

11 **Listen and number from 1 to 6 the types of music you are going to hear.**

... jazz

... rock'n'roll

... gospel

... rap

... blues

... pop music

Un peu de rattrapage

1. Formation du présent simple et du prétérit simple.

► Aide : mémento, n°17 et 18

■ Complète ce tableau avec le verbe *say*.

	PRESENT SIMPLE	PRETERIT SIMPLE
forme affirmative	I	I ....
	He	He ....
	They	They ....
forme négative	I	I ....
	He	He ....
	They	They ....
forme interrogative	.... I .... ?	.... I .... ?
	.... he .... ?	.... he .... ?
	.... they .... ?	.... they .... ?

2. Formation du présent et du prétérit en *be + -ing*.

► Aide : mémento, n°16

■ Complète le tableau en mettant les verbes au prétérit en *be + -ing*.

It isn't raining.	....
Is he doing his homework?	....
Why aren't you listening?	....
What's going on?	....
They're wearing funny hats.	....

3. Les années. ► Aide : mémento, n°1

A Ecris ces années en toutes lettres :

1861 ....

1901 ....

1955 ....

2007..

B Que signifie en français :

the 1960s / the 60s : ....

the mid-50s : ....

the early 2000s : ....

the late 60s : ....

C Commente ces périodes en utilisant les expressions mentionnées ci-dessus.

1990-1999 : ....

1994-1996 : ....

1990-1993 : ....

1997-1999 : ....

Basics

1 When did both of them become famous?

► pages 14-15

1. Ask questions. ► page 14

A Lis ces réponses puis complète les questions qui leur correspondent dans le tableau ci-dessous. Lorsqu'il n'y a pas de mot interrogatif, de verbe ou d'éléments après le verbe, barre la case.

1. No, his parents were not wealthy (*aisés*).
2. Yes, he did. In 1967. But he divorced two years later.
3. In the late 50s.
4. He sold about five million records.
5. No, he wasn't. He was a rock singer.
6. Of a heart attack.
7. He was only 42.

mot interrogatif	auxiliaire	sujet	verbe	
1.	....	....	....	wealthy ?
2.	....	....	....	.... ?
3.	....	....	....	popular ?
4. .... records	....	....	....	.... ?
5.	....	....	....	a jazz singer ?
6. How	....	....	....	.... ?
7.	....	....	....	when .... ?

REMEMBER
Au prétérit simple : les questions se forment avec l'auxiliaire .... suivi d'un verbe en base verbale.
Exemple : ....
Lorsque l'on conjugue le verbe *be*, on emploie seulement .... / .... qui servent à la fois d'auxiliaire et de verbe.
Exemple : ....

B Traduis les questions suivantes :

1. Quand es-tu arrivé ? Qui as-tu rencontré ?

   ....

2. Pourquoi n'étais-tu pas à la maison ?

   ....

C Complète le texte suivant avec des verbes au prétérit à la forme affirmative ou négative.

Elvis Presley .... American. He .... born in Mississippi but he .... up there; he .... up in Tennessee.
He .... his career at the age of 16 and soon .... very popular. He .... very talented.
He .... music at school but he .... the guitar very well. He .... his own songs. His fans .... him the King.
He .... a large family, he only .... one daughter. He .... long: he .... only 42 when he ....

2. Group work. ► page 14

Pose des questions à l'autre groupe pour remplir la grille ci-dessus.

	Bob Marley	**John Lennon**
Personal Data		
1. Date of birth.	....	....
2. Place of birth.	....	....
3. Date of death.	....	....
4. The way he died.	....	....
5. Where he grew up.	....	....
6. Married?	....	....
7. Children? How many?	....	....
Singing Career		
1. Musical education.	....	....
2. Beginning of career.	....	....
3. Name of his group.	....	....
4. Date of break-up.	....	....
5. Composer?	....	....
6. Type of music he sang.	....	....
7. Titles of two most famous songs.	....	....

3. Make comments. ► page 15

■ **A l'aide de la grille page 7, complète ces phrases en utilisant "Both of them ..." :**

1. .... at the age of sixteen.
2. .... their own songs.
3. .... , Bob Marley in 1966 and John Lennon in 1969.
4. .... young: John Lennon was 40 and Bob Marley was 36.

Oral practice

► page 15

REMEMBER

La terminaison *–ic* entraîne un accent sur la syllabe qui précède.

Exemples : ....

Exceptions : CATHOLIC • ARABIC • POLITICS

■ **Voici d'autres mots avec la terminaison *–ic* : souligne les syllabes accentuées.**

ARTIST → ARTISTIC ACROBAT → ACROBATIC REALIST → REALISTIC

HISTORY → HISTORIC ALLERGY → ALLERGIC ENERGY → ENERGETIC

Tu constates que cette terminaison est « forte » car elle peut entraîner un déplacement d'accent de mot par rapport à l'accentuation du mot de base.

Listening

► page 15

1. Listening comprehension.

A

1. When was the concert? ....
2. How long did it last? ....
3. Who went to the concert? Andy ☐ Jennifer ☐ Mark ☐
4. Andy is surprised. Why? ....
5. Some people outside were selling tickets. Yes ☐ No ☐

B

6. Mark bought a ticket ☐ didn't buy a ticket ☐.
7. Jennifer bought a ticket ☐ didn't buy a ticket ☐.
   Why ? Because ....

C

8. A woman had a spare ticket because ....

9. She sold it ☐ gave it ☐ to Jennifer.

10. The seat was ☐ wasn't ☐ a very good one.

D

11. Andy is angry ☐ lucky ☐ surprised ☐.
Mark was angry ☐ lucky ☐ surprised ☐.
Jennifer was angry ☐ lucky ☐ surprised ☐.

E **Dictation.**

1. ....
2. ....
3. ....

2. Summary.

....

....

....

....

....

....

....

Basics

2 What was going on? What happened?

► pages 16-17

1. What was going on? ► page 16

Observe ces images montrant ce que chaque membre de la famille MacArthur faisait au même moment ce matin à 7 heures. Complète les phrases ci-dessous au prétérit en *be* + *-ing*.

[get dressed]

[walk the dog]

[have a shower]

[shave]

[feed the cat]

[have breakfast]

1. While Eileen was having a shower, Alex ....

2. While John .... , ...

3. While Tom ....

4. While Mark..

5. While Alex ....

6. While Susie ....

UNIT 1

2. What happened? ►page 17

A Observe les phrases suivantes :

*While **I was listening** (1) to the radio, my mobile **rang** (2).*
*When my mobile **rang** (3), **I turned off** (4) the radio.*

• Quels verbes sont au prétérit simple ? 1 ☐ 2 ☐ 3 ☐ 4 ☐
• Quels verbes sont au prétérit en *be* +-*ing* ? 1 ☐ 2 ☐ 3 ☐ 4 ☐
• Quels verbes évoquent :
- une activité en cours à un moment donné du passé ? 1 ☐ 2 ☐ 3 ☐ 4 ☐
- un « événement » interrompant une activité en cours ? 1 ☐ 2 ☐ 3 ☐ 4 ☐
- deux « événements » consécutifs ? 1 ☐ 2 ☐ 3 ☐ 4 ☐

REMEMBER
• Pour parler d'un événement ou d'une succession d'événements, j'utilise le prétérit ....
Exemple : ....
• Pour parler d'une activité en cours interrompue par un événement, j'utilise .... (l'activité en cours), ... (l'événement).
Exemple : ....

B Complète les phrases avec *was, were* ou *did*.

1. What .... you doing when I phoned?
2. What .... you do when she fainted?
3. He fell while he .... climbing up a tree.
4. We .... not hear the bell because everyone .... screaming.
5. What .... you say? Sorry, I .... not listening.

C Complète les phrases par un des verbes de la liste au prétérit simple ou au prétérit en *be* + -*ing*.

• arrive • ask • clap • go • hear • play • rip • run • see • start • take • watch

1. When the band .... on the stage, the audience .... their hands and .... to scream.
2. While I .... pictures of the singer, he .... off his T-shirt.
3. After the concert, the fans .... behind stage and .... the musicians for autographs.
4. While we .... the concert on TV, our parents .... cards. But all of a sudden, we .... a loud noise outside. So, we all .... outside but we .... anything.

3. Listen. ►page 17

Coche la réponse qui te semble juste.

	1.	2.	3.	4.	5.	6.
a						
b						

4. Reported speech. ►page 17

A Observe ces phrases :

(1) *Ted to Lucy: "I'll give **you my** phone number."*
*Ted says that **he**'ll give **her his** phone number.*

(2) *Lucy to Ted: "I'll give **you my** phone number, too."*
*Lucy says that **she**'ll give **him her** phone number, too.*

Tu remarques que le passage au style indirect peut entraîner un **changement de référent** (*la personne dont on parle*) : il est alors nécessaire de modifier les pronoms personnels ainsi que les adjectifs et pronoms possessifs. Il faut donc bien repérer qui parle, à qui et de qui.

B Rapporte au style indirect ces courts dialogues en veillant à modifier correctement les mots en gras : ► mémento n°3 et 4

Andy — The CD Sarah offered **me** for **my** birthday is fantastic.
Andy's mother — **You** may be right but **I** don't want **you** to listen to music while **you** are doing **your** homework.

Andy says that ……………………………………………………………………………

……………………………………………………………………………………………

Andy's mother says that ……………………………………………………………………

……………………………………………………………………………………………

Clara — **I**'m not allowed to go to concerts with **my** sister. **Our** father thinks **we** are too young. He doesn't understand **us**.
Ralph — **Mine** is much more understanding than **yours**.

Clara ……………………………………………………………………………………

……………………………………………………………………………………………

Ralph ……………………………………………………………………………………

Oral practice ► page 17

A Ecris les signes de liaison dans les groupes de mots suivants.

• grow up • sort of music • his own songs • both of us • neither of us

B Fais de même dans le texte suivant, et souligne également les mots qui sont accentués.

While the band was playing, people in the audience were dancing. Ted fell in love with Lucy. All of a sudden the lights went out and he took her hand.

 ► page 17

1. Listening comprehension.

A

1. Lisa is happy for her Mum. ☐
sorry for her Mum. ☐
anxious about her Mum. ☐

2. She's talking about last night ☐ the other night ☐ every night ☐.

B

3. Lisa's Mum says ....

4. Tom believes it ☐ doesn't believe it ☐.
Lisa believes it ☐ doesn't believe it ☐.

C

5. What were their parents doing? When and where?

Who?	*When?*	*What?*	*Where?*
Lisa's Mum	....	....	....
Tom's Dad	....	....	....

6. Tom suggests that ....

D

7. What happened to the singer? ....
the guitarist? ....
the drummer (*le batteur*)? ....

8. Lisa is embarrassed ☐ embarrassing ☐.

E Report what they say.

1. Lisa says that ....
2. She says that ....
....
3. Tom says that ....
....

2. Summary.

....
....
....
....
....
....
....

3 They looked at each other. ► page 18

1. The beginning of a love story.

A Observe ces dessins et leur légende.

No, they are not talking to themselves! *They are talking to each other.*

• ***each other*** est :
un pronom réfléchi (renvoie au sujet) ☐ un pronom réciproque (renvoie à l'autre) ☐

• ***themselves*** est :
un pronom réfléchi (renvoie au sujet) ☐ un pronom réciproque (renvoie à l'autre) ☐

B Complète les phrases en utilisant le pronom réfléchi qui convient. ► mémento n°5

1. They fell down and hurt ....
2. She didn't have a photo of ....
3. The candidates introduced .... at the beginning of the meeting.
4. The concert was great! We really enjoyed ....
5. Be careful! Don't burn .... ; it's very hot!
6. Well, the story .... was interesting but I didn't like the style of the writer.

C Complète les phrases en trouvant un verbe suivi de *each other*.

1. — Can you think of two people who .... very much?
   — Yes! Romeo and Juliet.
2. We always .... presents for Christmas.
3. My dog and my cat get on well: they always .... with ....
4. — Do you still keep in touch with your friend from Chile?
   — Sure! We .... emails to .... twice a week.

More Words

▶ page 19

1. Hidden words.

■ **Find seven words from the list that are hidden in the instruments of the band.**

....
....
....
....
....
....
....

2. A musician.

■ **Complete the following text with the words from the list.**

I play the violin, but I don't play classical music. So I play and in a .... not in an ....
My brother plays the piano very well, so he is at the .... and he also composes the .... of our songs. My girlfriend is the .... It's rather unusual for a girl, but she's very good at it! She's got a real sense of .... We give concerts, but unfortunately we haven't got any .... of them. Sometimes it's difficult to combine this with my studies because we .... twice a week. In fact, I have a .... right now.

3. Coin New Words.

Remarques sur la formation des adverbes:

1. modifications orthographiques :
easy → *easily* *horrible* → *horribly* *basic* → *basically*

2. les mots terminés par *-ly* ne sont pas tous des adverbes.
lovely • *friendly* • *silly* • *lonely* sont des .... ;
early • *daily* • *monthly* • *weekly* peuvent être adverbes ou adjectifs.

■ **Complete the grid.**

adjective	adverb	
incredible	.... :	....
....	usually :	....
....	.... :	*tranquillement*
noisy	.... :	....
fortunate	.... :	....
fluent	.... :	....
....	.... :	*avec succès*

Topic

Becoming a pop star ► pages 20-21

1. Comprehension. ► page 20

A Introduction.

1. Who participates in these programmes? ....
2. Who makes pop stars out of them? ....
3. Who votes? How often? ....
4. Who goes on tour and records an album? ....

B Paragraphs 1, 2 and 3: Justify the following sentences quoting from the text.
(Justifie les phrases suivantes en citant le texte)

1. David had never studied music before.
....
2. All the other contestants were more experienced than him.
....
3. He realized he was not as good as the others.
....
4. He was eliminated in less than a month.
....
5. He was busy working all day long.
....
6. He had to exercise every day.
....
7. Rehearsals and live shows were very tiring.
....
8. He was very nervous on the day of the vote.
....
9. He was not surprised when he was eliminated.
....
10. Most boys didn't vote for him.
....

C Paragraphs 4 and 5: Complete the following sentences.

1. The group began to crack because..
....
2. David benefited from this experience because ....
....
....
3. He realized that to become a star, it is important to ....
....
and to ....

2. Find the English for:

• plusieurs : ....
• parmi : ....
• téléspectateur : ....
• je m'y attendais : ....
• un moment dur : ....
• au fur et à mesure que le temps passait : ....
• ma famille me manquait beaucoup : ....
• grâce à : ....
• par-dessus tout : ....
• une volonté de fer : ....
¥confiance en soi : ....

3. Linking word. ▸ page 21

I knew that girls supported me ***whereas*** *most boys didn't.*

A Match each linking word with its translation.

whereas •	• *c'est pourquoi*
since •	• *alors que, au contraire*
that's why •	• *puisque*

B Connect the phrases in A and B with one linking word and complete the grid.

A		B
1. David wasn't surprised when he was eliminated,	**that's why**	**1.** they got on well at the beginning.
2. He lived far from home,		**2.** he sometimes missed his family.
3. The candidates have to keep fit,	**since**	**3.** he knew he was a bit behind.
4. At the end the group cracked,		**4.** they have to exercise every day.
5. He didn't have any musical training,	**whereas**	**5.** other contestants did.

A1 .... B.......	A2 .... B.......	A3 .... B.......
A4 .... B.......	A5 .... B.......	

4. Reading aloud. ▸ page 21

■ Get ready to read this part of the text aloud*.

While I was waiting for the results of the votes
my heart was pounding, I was trembling and sweating.
And when I heard my name, I was disappointed
but I was expecting it: I knew that girls supported me,
whereas most boys didn't.

*pour t'aider, ajoute les signes de liaison et souligne les mots accentués.

UNIT 1

5. Writing task. ► page 21

Your favourite contestant was eliminated.
You think that it was unfair and you write a letter to protest.

Quelques conseils.

Reporte-toi à la rubrique *Savoir écrire une lettre* de la partie *Outils méthodologiques* de ton manuel (pages 132-133) pour t'assurer de la bonne présentation de ta lettre et des formules appropriées.

ton adresse
date

nom de la chaîne et de l'émission
adresse fictive ou retrouvée sur Internet

formule de début

introduction :
Explique le motif de ta lettre (sentiments et raisons).
- *I…* **(présent *be* + *-ing*)** *… to express / to tell you / to let you know …*
- *I am angry / furious / revolted, because …* **(prétérit)**

contenu : (présent)

- arguments en faveur de ton / ta candidat(e) :
• *good / best dancer / singer* • *energy* • *strong will to win* • *hard-working*
• *sporty* • *good-looking* • *friendly* • *funny* • *good mood* • *self-control*
• *talented* • *different / unusual voice* • *imaginative* • *cool …*

- opinion sur un ou les autre(s) candidat(es) :
• *not as … as* • *less / more … than* • *pretentious* • *vulgar*
• *self-confident* • *boastful* • *jealous* • *big-headed …*

- opinion sur les autres téléspectateurs :
• *bad taste* • *no artistic sense* • *conformist* • *reject what's new* • *influenced …*

conclusion :

- une décision :
• *never vote again* • *never watch … again* **(futur)**

- une demande :
• *ask his / her address*

et la raison de cette demande :
• *send encouraging message* • *tell him / her that …*

formule de fin
signature
nom

More about...

... songs rooted in rebellion ▸ pages 22-23

1. General comprehension.

A Complete the grid.

Which movement	When it appeared	Where it started	Artists mentioned
....	....	the USA	- .... - ....
....	....	....	- ....
....	....	....	- ....
rap	....	....	- .... - ....

B Match the movements and their slogans, then answer the questions.

Protest songs •	• *No Future*
Reggae •	• *Peace and Love*
Punk •	• *Stand up for your rights*

Which types of music originated in poor areas? ....
Which types of music shocked the audiences? ....

2. Detailed comprehension.

A All these sentences are wrong. Correct them by quoting the text.

Protest songs

1. The protest songs of the 60s were against WWII.
....

2. Their message was very pessimistic about the future.
....

3. The Woodstock festival was not a success.
....

Reggae

4. Rastafarianism is a Jamaican political party.
....

5. Rastafarians do not believe in God.
....

B What or who do these expressions refer to?

Punk music

1. The types of music punks hated. ....
2. A serious problem in Britain during the 70s. ....
3. Someone who isn't human, according to the Sex Pistols. ....

Rap

4. Feelings expressed through rap. ....
5. People that are criticized in rap songs. ....

QUIZ

► pages 26-27

How much do you know about the United States of America?

1 In the USA there are:

- more than 500 million inhabitants ☐
- about 300 million inhabitants ☐
- less than 200 million inhabitants ☐

2 The USA is:

- 5 times as big as France ☐
- 17 times as big as France ☐
- 50 times as big as France ☐

3 The US has borders with:

Mexico ☐ Brazil ☐
Chile ☐ Canada ☐

4 The Rocky Mountains are:

in the west ☐ in the east ☐

The Appalachians are:

in the west ☐ in the east ☐

5 Match the states and their capitals:

state	*state capital*
New York •	• Sacramento
Washington •	• Tallahassee
California •	• Olympia
Florida •	• Albany

6 Which name doesn't refer to both a state and a river?

Missouri ☐ Mississippi ☐
Arkansas ☐ Ohio ☐
Sacramento ☐ Colorado ☐

7 Can you find cities or states with:

a Spanish name: • ....
• ....

a French name: • ....
• ....

an Indian name: • ....
• ....

8 Cross the odd man out:

North Carolina South Carolina
Mexico New Mexico
Virginia West Virginia

9 The first English immigrants settled in:

Georgia ☐ Virginia ☐ Louisiana ☐

10 The USA became an independent nation in:

1620 ☐ 1776 ☐ 1865 ☐

11 The first president of the USA was:

Lincoln ☐ Roosevelt ☐
Washington ☐ Kennedy ☐

12 Two American presidents died the same way:

- Washington and Roosevelt ☐
- Lincoln and Roosevelt ☐
- Lincoln and Kennedy ☐

13 One of the causes of the Civil War was:

- the attack of Pearl Harbour ☐
- the Great Depression ☐
- slavery ☐

14 There was a major financial crisis in:

1789 ☐ 1929 ☐ 1939 ☐

15 Demonstrations against the war in Vietnam took place:

- in the 50s ☐
- in the 60s ☐
- in the 90s ☐

Un peu de rattrapage

1. Les question-tags.

A Lis les bulles ci-dessous puis remplis le texte qui suit.

It's pretty cold, ***isn't it?***

They arrived very late, ***didn't they ?***

She never agrees, ***does she?***

You like peanut butter, ***don't you?***

You didn't call me, ***did you?***

• Les *question-tags* se forment comme une question :
en commençant par un .... suivi d'un ....

• Ils reprennent l'auxiliaire de la phrase sous sa forme contraire :

quand le verbe est :	**le *question-tag* est :**
à la forme affirmative	à la forme ....
à la forme négative	à la forme ....
avec *never*	à la forme ....

• Dans deux cas le verbe n'a pas d'auxiliaire apparent : aux formes affirmatives du présent simple et du prétérit simple. On reprend alors les auxiliaires *don't, doesn't* ou *didn't.*

Exemples : ....
....

B Complète les phrases suivantes :

1. There are 50 states in the US, ...
2. Slavery was abolished in 1865, ...
3. The Americans entered WWII in 1941, ...
4. The Statue of Liberty has become a symbol of the US, ...
5. The Americans don't have the same accent as the British, ...
6. The first English settlers didn't settle in the west, ...
7. The Americans vote every four years for their President, ...
8. It never snows in Death Valley, ...
9. You can't see the Statue of Liberty from Central Park, ...

2. La lecture des nombres. ► Aide : mémento, n°1

Ecris en toutes lettres :

• les nombres suivants :
296 : ....
4,343 : ....
120,000 : ....
290,000,000 : ....

• les proportions suivantes :
1/10 : .... 1/2 : ....
50% : .... 3/4 : ....

Basics

1 There are so many skyscrapers! ► pages 28-29

1. Ask questions. ► page 28

A Quelles expressions utilise-t-on pour obtenir les renseignements suivants ? Recopie-les dans la grille. Attention : Certaines expressions peuvent être utilisées plusieurs fois.

• *how much* • *how many* • *how old* • *how high* • *how long* • *how hot* • *how cold* • *how far*

number of …		weight	
temperature in January		length	
temperature in July		distance	
age		time to get to …	
height		price	

B Note ici les réponses aux questions posées.

New York City		The Statue of Liberty		The Empire State Building	
number of boroughs		age		height	
number of inhabitants		height		number of floors	
number of nationalities		weight		number of steps	
temperature in January		length of its arm		number of elevators	
temperature in July		length of its index		time to get to the top	
		length of its nose		price of a ticket	
		distance from Manhattan		number of people working inside	
		time to get there			

C Manhattan.

• Ecris sur la carte le nom de chacun des lieux mentionnés ci-dessous.

Central Park is the biggest park in Manhattan.

Broadway is the longest avenue in Manhattan, running the entire length of the island.

5th Avenue, New York's most prestigious avenue, divides Manhattan between the west side and the east side.

The Empire State Building, situated at the corner of 5th Avenue and W. 34th Street, is one of the best-known and most visited buildings in the world.

The Metropolitan Museum of Art, built in Central Park, is one of the largest museums in the world. Its entrance is on 5th Avenue.

Harlem, situated in northern Manhattan, is home to the largest population of New York's African American and Hispanic communities.

Ellis Island is a small island to the south of Manhattan where immigrants landed before entering America.

The Statue of Liberty is located on a tiny island, south of Ellis Island.

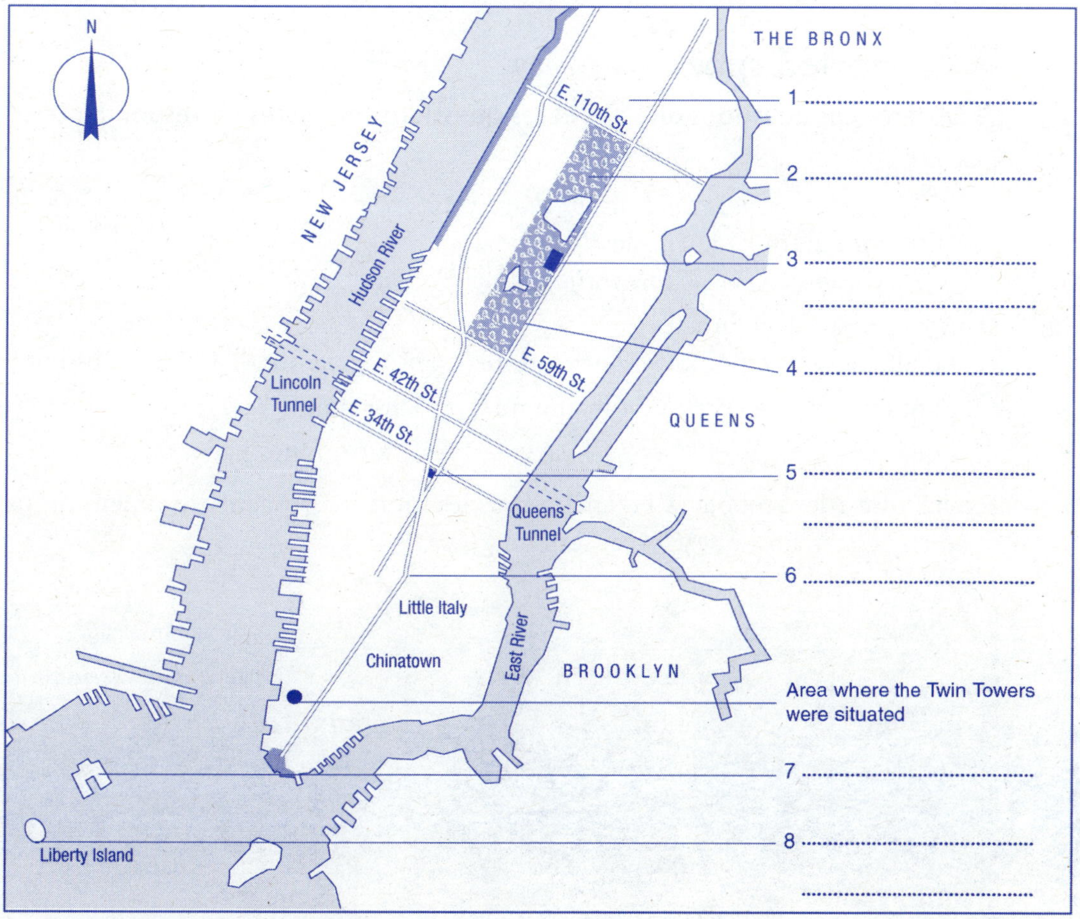

• Relève tous les adjectifs au superlatif.

....

....

• Quel est l'adjectif de base de *"the best-known"*? ....

2. Pairwork. ► page 29

REMEMBER

so *spectacular*	***so*** *tiring*	
so many *avenues*	***so many*** *skyscrapers*	***so many*** *tourists*
so much *pollution*	***so much*** *traffic*	***so much*** *rain*

- ***so*** est suivi d'un ....
- ***so many*** est suivi d'un nom indénombrable ☐ dénombrable pluriel ☐.
- ***so much*** est suivi d'un nom indénombrable ☐ dénombrable pluriel ☐.

Complète les phrases par *so, so much* ou *so many*.

1. There are .... countries I would like to visit. But I can't: travelling is .... expensive!
2. There was .... noise in the hotel that no one could sleep.
3. Have you ever seen .... snow in November?
4. I was .... tired after the interview: I had to answer .... questions on .... subjects!
5. I spent .... money on souvenirs!

3. Reported speech. ► page 29

A Observe ces questions directes et les questions indirectes correspondantes.

1. ***"When do shops close?"***
→ *The tourists want to know* ***when shops close****.*
2. ***"Does this train go*** *to Harlem?"*
→ *They want to know* ***if this train goes*** *to Harlem.*

Dans les questions indirectes :
- les guillemets et le point d'interrogation sont maintenus ☐ disparaissent ☐;
- le mot interrogatif (WH-) est maintenu ☐ disparaît ☐;
- les questions sans WH- (*yes / no questions*) sont introduites par ....

Remarque : le symbole WH- inclut tous les mots interrogatifs commençant par ces deux lettres ainsi que *How* et ses composés.

REMEMBER

	question en WH-	***yes / no question***
question directe	WH- + **auxiliaire** + **sujet** + **verbe** Exemple :	**auxiliaire** + **sujet** + **verbe** Exemple : ....
question indirecte	WH- + **sujet** + **verbe** Exemple : *They want to know*	*if* + **sujet** + **verbe** Exemple : *They want to know* ....

B Transformе ces questions directes en questions indirectes introduites par *I'd like to know* :

1. Is the Mississippi the longest river in the world?

....

2. How many time zones are there in the USA?

....

3. Where did the Pilgrims sail from?

....

4. Was Abraham Lincoln assassinated during the Civil War?

....

....

5. Why is NewYork also called "the Big Apple"?

....

6. When did Hawaii become the 50th state of America?

....

7. When did Napoleon sell Louisiana to the Americans?

....

Oral practice

► page 29

REMEMBER

La terminaison *-ion* – comme la terminaison *-ic* – entraîne une accentuation sur la syllabe qui ....

Exemples : ....

Exception : TELEVISION

D'après les règles d'accentuation que tu as vues dans les unités 1 et 2, tu sais repérer les syllabes accentuées dans les mots suivants. Souligne-les et entraîne-toi à les lire.

CONVERSATION	INFORMATION	ATOMIC	DECLARATION
MILLION	SEGREGATION	DEMONSTRATION	HISPANIC
ASSASSINATION	AUTOMATIC	SUSPENSION	

Listening

► page 29

1. Listening comprehension.

A

1. Gemma is pleased ☐ annoyed ☐ excited ☐
   because the queue is ....
2. After the visit she wants to ....
   What for? To ....
3. She can do it tomorrow. Yes ☐ No ☐
   Why? Because ....

B

4. The shops close at .... o'clock.
5. Gemma needs: 🕐 ☐ 🕐 ☐ 🕐 🕐 ☐
6. Mark thinks she will have enough time. Yes ☐ No ☐

C

7. Gemma wants to go to the top. ☐ She wants to leave. ☐
   Why? Because .... and ....
8. Mark agrees ☐ doesn't agree ☐.
   Why or why not?
   ....

D

9. Mark has never been up to the top. ☐
   has been up to the top once. ☐
   has been up to the top more than once. ☐
10. Gemma is surprised. She says, "So, you ...."
    She is thankful ☐ disappointed ☐.
11. Mark is Gemma's ....

E Report what they say.

1. Gemma asks ....
2. She wants to know ....
3. Mark asks her ....
4. Gemma asks him ....

2. Summary.

....
....
....
....
....
....
....
....

Basics

2 This is the first time I've been to the West Coast! ► pages 30-31

1. Look and comment. ► page 30

Mélanie doit partir en week-end chez Amanda et a noté tout ce qu'elle doit faire avant de partir. Commente ce qu'elle a déjà fait (ce qui est coché) et ce qu'elle n'a pas encore fait.

tidy my room
✓ finish my French essay
buy a present for Amanda's parents
call Tom
✓ check the time of the train
✓ buy a new swimsuit

1. ....
2. ....
3. ....
4. ....
5. ....
6. ....

2. Make dialogues. ► page 30

A Souligne dans ce texte les verbes au prétérit et au *present perfect*, et classe-les dans le tableau ci-dessous.

– Colin, is this the first time you have been to the States?
– No, I have been here on many occasions before! Six years ago, when I was a student, I spent a year in California. Then I worked for an American firm for three years. I have travelled all over the United States but this is the first time I have flown over New York in a helicopter.

Prétérit	*Present perfect*
....	....
....	....
....	....
	....

REMEMBER
• Le .... traduit un événement passé, terminé, daté.
Exemple : ....
• Le .... traduit le bilan de ses expériences faites ou non faites, et non datées.
Exemple : ....

B ***This is the first time I have flown over New York.***

• **Quelle est la traduction de ce titre?**
C'est la première fois que je survole New York. ☐
C'est la première fois que j'ai survolé New York. ☐

• **Pourquoi est-il logique d'utiliser le *present perfect* dans ce cas ?**
....

• **Classe ces expressions de temps suivantes dans le tableau ci-dessous.**
• *three days ago* • *ever* • *yesterday* • *up to now* (jusqu'à maintenant) • *last Thursday*
• *in the sixties* • *it is the first time* • *the day before yesterday* (avant-hier)

S'emploient avec un verbe au prétérit	S'emploient avec un verbe au *present perfect*
....	....

C Complète les phrases ci-dessous avec les verbes proposés en utilisant le prétérit ou le *present perfect*.

1. – .... you .... your trip to England when you...................... in primary school? [enjoy ; be]
   – Well, I think I was too young: I .... homesick, I .... my family very much. [feel ; miss]
2. – .... he .... this car before? [drive]
   – Yes, he .... ! It is not the first time he .... his father's car. [take]
3. – Do you know who the singer is?
   – No, I don't; but it is the third time I .... this song on the radio. [hear]
4. – What .... last night? [happen]
   – Her car .... and she .... walk home. [break down ; have to]
5. We have a very old computer at home. But up to now we .... any problem with it. [not have]

3. Listen and comment. ►page 31

Ecoute et coche la bonne case, puis commente les situations à l'aide des verbes proposés.

	1	2	3	4	5
It's the first time ...					
It's not the first time ...					
	[read]	[taste]	[see]	[eat]	[take a plane]

Oral practice

► page 31

A Les pronoms personnels accentués :
Ecoute plusieurs séries de phrases et coche celles qui signifient :

1. Et toi, as-tu déjà fait du surf? a. ☐ b. ☐
2. Moi, je n'ai jamais voyagé à l'étranger. a. ☐ b. ☐
3. Elle, elle ne veut pas venir. a. ☐ b. ☐
4. Nous, on reste ici. a. ☐ b. ☐
5. Elles, elles vont partir plus tôt. a. ☐ b. ☐

B Autres mots accentués : Tu vas entendre quatre fois la même phrase. Souligne à chaque fois le mot mis en relief puis commente oralement le sens exact de chaque phrase.

1. I have cleaned my desk.
2. I have cleaned my desk.
3. I have cleaned my desk.
4. I have cleaned my desk.

Listening

► page 31

1. Listening comprehension.

A

1. Helen won .... dollars.
2. Today is the luckiest day of her life. Yes ☐ No ☐
3. Helen is a gambler ☐ an inexperienced gambler ☐.
4. She helped someone. ☐ Someone helped her. ☐
   Who? ....

B

5. She played .... time(s).
   She won ....time(s).

C

6. She stopped because it was beginning to be ....
   that she ....
7. Jeremy thinks it was a good idea to stop. Yes ☐ No ☐

D

8. Helen decides to ....
9. Then Jeremy realizes that someone has stolen ☐ damaged ☐ their car.
10. Both of them are calm ☐ devastated (*catastrophés*) ☐ don't care ☐.
11. The repairs will cost about .... dollars.
12. With the money they're going to ....

E Dictation.

1. ....
2. ....
3. ....

2. Summary.

....
....
....
....
....
....
....

Basics

3 Carrie is on vacation in the South. So is Jeff. ► page 32

1. Listen and speak. ► page 32

A Observe les phrases ci-dessous.

(1a) *Carrie **is** on vacation in the South.* (1b) ***So is** Jeff.*
(2a) *She **hasn't** been to the South before.* (2b) ***Neither has** Jeff.*
(3a) *She **visited** some old houses in New Orleans.* (3b) ***So did** Jeff.*

Les phrases **(b)** expriment une différence ☐ une similitude ☐ entre Carrie et Jeff.

B Traduis en français.

So is Jeff. → ....
Neither has Jeff. → ....
So did Jeff. → ....

REMEMBER

Pour exprimer une **similitude** :

• à la suite d'une **phrase affirmative** on emploie :
So ☐ ***Neither*** ☐ + l'auxiliaire de reprise suivi du sujet.
Exemple : ....

• à la suite d'une **phrase négative** on emploie :
So ☐ ***Neither*** ☐ + l'auxiliaire de reprise suivi du sujet.
Exemple : ....

C Exprime les points communs entre les personnages suivants :

1. Ted has taken lots of photos in Las Vegas. .... Mary.
2. Bob Marley composed his own songs. .... John Lennon.
3. Steve was singing along with the music. .... his friends.
4. Fred wouldn't want to miss the concert. .... Clara.
5. My friend and I have never been abroad. .... my best friend.
6. Dave is a contestant in a TV programme.
He needs a lot of energy. .... the others.
He is trying to be the finalist. .... the others.
He'll never participate again. .... the others.

2. Make comments. ► page 32

A Observe les phrases ci-dessous.

(1a) *Kevin* ***enjoys*** *staying at home.* (1b) *Vince* ***doesn't****!*
(2a) *Kevin* ***isn't*** *adventurous.* (2b) *Vince* ***is****!*
(3a) *Kevin* ***has*** *never* ***travelled*** *abroad.* (3b) *Vince* ***has****!*

Les phrases **(b)** expriment une différence ☐ une similitude ☐ entre Kevin et Vince.

REMEMBER

Pour exprimer la **différence** :

- à la suite d'une **phrase affirmative**, on utilise un auxiliaire à la forme ....
- à la suite d'une **phrase négative**, on utilise un auxiliaire à la forme ....

B Utilise les éléments donnés dans la colonne "Kevin" pour compléter les phrases qui concernent Vince.

Vince	Kevin
• Vince .... abroad lots of times.	• Kevin hasn't.
• He .... his time watching TV.	• Kevin does.
• At school he .... in geography and he was good at it.	• Kevin wasn't.
• He .... lots of books about explorers when he was a boy.	• Kevin didn't.
• So now he .... to sail all around the world.	• Kevin wouldn't.

3. Listen and speak. ► page 32

Écoute et coche la case qui correspond à ton cas personnel.

	1	2	3	4	5	5	7	8
the same								
different								

More Words

▶ page 33

1. Hidden words. ▶ page 33

■ Place twenty-one words from the list in the grid.

2. British English and American English.

■ What do the Americans and the English say in the following situations?

1. *Quelqu'un veut aller au centre ville; on lui conseille de prendre le métro ou un taxi.*

In the USA
"How do I get .... ?"
"Take ....
or .... "

In Great Britain
"How do I get to the .... ?"
"Take ....
or .... "

2. *Un camionneur qui est sur l'autoroute doit faire le plein d'essence pour son camion.*

In the USA
The .... - driver on
the ....
needs ....

In Great Britain
The .... - driver on
the ....
needs ....

3. *Quelqu'un ne prend jamais l'ascenseur pour monter dans son appartement.*

In the USA
"My ....
is on the first floor, so I never take
the ...."

In Great Britain
"My ....
is on the ground floor, so I never take
the ...."

3. Coin New Words. ► page 33

A Find the opposites of the following adjectives and fill in the grid. You can check your answers in a dictionary.

• usual • fair • pleasant • responsible • mature • direct • identified • accessible • lucky • safe

ir-	
im-	
in-	
un-	

B What is the English for :

- injuste : ....
- dangereux : ....
- inhabituel : ....
- non-identifié : ....
- désagréable : ....
- qui n'a pas de chance : ....

Topic

A school in Harlem ► pages 34-35

1. Comprehension. ► page 34

Introduction.

1. The school is located in a disadvantaged neighborhood. right ☐ wrong ☐

....

....

2. The population in Harlem is multiracial. right ☐ wrong ☐

....

Paragraph 1.

3. Harlem is like the rest of Manhattan. right ☐ wrong ☐

....

....

4. Children from Harlem have everything they want. right ☐ wrong ☐

....

Paragraph 2.

5. They fight because they're angry. right ☐ wrong ☐

....

6. Parents encourage their children to defend themselves. right ☐ wrong ☐

....

....

Paragraph 3.

7. They have to show they are not intimidated. right ☐ wrong ☐

....

8. If they refuse to fight, they think they will look ridiculous. right ☐ wrong ☐

....

Paragraph 4.

9. Music and Art are the most important subjects. right ☐ wrong ☐

....

10. Discipline is very strict. right ☐ wrong ☐

....

....

....

11. The teachers know that many of their students have a difficult life outside school. right ☐ wrong ☐

....

Paragraph 5.

12. Only students from Harlem go to this school. right ☐ wrong ☐

....

....

13. Lots of students leave school before they finish their studies. right ☐ wrong ☐

....

14. Many students have succeeded in their studies. right ☐ wrong ☐

....

2. Find the English for:

- différent de : ....
- C'est un monde à part : ....
- tellement de choses : ....
- la colère : ....
- même les parents disent ... : ....
- menacer : ....
- Que voulez vous dire? : ....
- Prenons un exemple : ....
- un couloir : ....
- l'informatique : ....
- les armes : ....
- ne pas obéir au règlement : ....
- douloureux : ....
- réussir : ....
- quelqu'un qui abandonne ses études : ....
- « Je reviens de loin » : ....

3. Linking word. ▶ page 35

*Harlem is in Manhattan **and yet** downtown*
Manhattan is such a different and inaccessible world.

A Match each linking word with its translation.

whereas •	• *et pourtant*
and yet •	• *donc*
so •	• *alors que, au contraire*

B Connect the phrases in A and B with one linking word and complete the grid.

A		B
1. Our school is located in Harlem,		**1.** many of our students continue their studies.
2. There are many things our kids can't have,	**whereas**	**2.** they feel frustrated.
3. There are many drop-outs in other schools,	**and yet**	**3.** it has attracted students from all over the city.
4. We are very strict about discipline,	**so**	**4.** we have specialized in these subjects.
5. Technology and computer science are very important for young people,		**5.** we have zero tolerance for fighting.

A1 .... B...	A2 .... B...	A3 .... B...
A4 .... B...	A5 .... B...	

4. Reading aloud.

■ **Get ready to read this part of the text aloud.**

Is Harlem really different from the rest of the city?
It's a world apart! Harlem is in Manhattan, and yet downtown Manhattan is such a different and inaccessible world! There are so many things that kids here can't have! That's why they feel a lot of anger and frustration.

5. Writing task.

A student was caught fighting. The Principal has asked to see the student's father or mother. Imagine what the three of them say in this scene.

Quelques conseils.

1. Il s'agit d'une conversation. Donne un nom aux personnages.
Va à la ligne à chaque changement de personnage et (ré)écris son nom.
Veille à l'équilibre des rôles : les trois personnages doivent s'exprimer.

2. Les personnages doivent exprimer leurs sentiments, leurs arguments, leurs réactions.
Tu trouveras les idées essentielles dans le tableau ci-dessous.

	the Principal	**the student**	**the parent**
arguments	*zero tolerance / reputation of the school / rules / bad example or influence* **(présent)**	• *reasons for fighting:* *bump into / threaten / call (me) names / in danger / not my fault / some very tough pupils* **(prétérit)** *it's the first time* **(present perfect)**	• *his / her child's personality* **(adjectifs)** • *behaviour at home* **(présent)** • *importance of school for his/her future*
feelings	*angry / disappointed / …*	*sorry / (feel) ashamed / irresponsible / …*	*surprised / annoyed / worried / angry / …*
reactions	*punishes and explains why*	*apologizes / promises*	*understands / (dis)agrees / apologizes*

3. Termine en indiquant la sanction prise par le principal. Mentionne les réactions qu'elle suscite .

Cela peut : - clore la conversation ;
- faire l'objet d'un commentaire de ta part.

4. N'oublie pas les mots de liaison : ***whereas, and yet, so.***

More about...

... the USA, a nation of immigrants ► pages 36-37

1. General comprehension.

Complete the following text.

The ancestors of all Americans came from different continents:
.... , ... , ... ,
.... ,
So every American citizen is .... of immigrants. That is why the USA was called a ".............................. ".

2. Detailed comprehension.

A Fill in the grid.

	The Amerindians	The Blacks	The Hispanics
Where they came from			
When they arrived			
How many there are today		*about 12 %*	
What they are also called			

B All these sentences are wrong. Correct them.

1. The descendants of the first English settlers are called native Americans.
....
2. The Pilgrims left England for economic reasons.
....
3. They settled in the southwest of the United States.
....
4. None of them survived the cold.
....
5. Thanksgiving is celebrated on the fourth of July.
....

C Complete the following sentences.

1. The first European immigrants arrived in the .... during .... or during ....
2. Most of them passed through ....

D Are these sentences true (T) or false (F)?

1. The first immigrants from China arrived in the 19th century.
2. They worked in cotton fields.
3. The second wave of Asian immigrants did not come from China.
4. Many immigrants from Asia settled in California.

	T	F
1		
2		
3		
4		

QUIZ

► pages 40-41

How much do you know about Canada?

1 The population of Canada is about:

1/10 of the population of the USA ☐

half of the population of the USA ☐

2 The red leaf on the Canadian flag is the leaf of:

a maple tree *(érable)* ☐ an oak *(chêne)* ☐

3 In Canada, you pay with:

US dollars ☐ Canadian dollars ☐

4 The capital of Canada is:

Toronto ☐ Ottawa ☐ Quebec ☐

5 All main cities are:

along the US border ☐

along the coasts ☐

6 The distance from Vancouver to Quebec is about:

4,000 miles (6,500 km) ☐

2,200 miles (4,500 km) ☐

7 The name of the city which is nearest to the Arctic Circle is:

Whitehorse ☐

Iqaluit ☐

Churchill ☐

8 The mountains on the west are:

the Highlands ☐

the Rocky Mountains ☐

9 Which group does not belong to "The First Nations"?

the Inuit ☐

the Amerindians ☐

the Quebeckers ☐

10 Canada was a province of France:

from 1534 to 1663 ☐

from 1663 to 1763 ☐

from 1663 to 1867 ☐

11 Who founded the city of Quebec?

Jacques Cartier ☐

Samuel de Champlain ☐

12 The British settled in Canada:

after the French ☐

before the French ☐

13 The name of the most recent territory of Canada is:

Nova Scotia ☐

Nunavut ☐

Saskatchewan ☐

14 The flag of Canada is:

less than fifty years old ☐

more than fifty years old ☐

more than a hundred years old ☐

15 Which of the two statements is true:

Most Canadians speak French. ☐

Most Canadians speak English. ☐

Un peu de rattrapage

UNIT 3

1. Pronoms personnels et adjectifs possessifs.

► Aide : mémento, n°3 et 4

A Des intrus se sont glissés dans chaque colonne. Chasse-les en les rayant.

adjectifs possessifs			pronoms personnels compléments			
ME	HIS	YOUR	HER	HIS	THEM	
IT	THEIR	HIM	HIM	US	MY	ITS
MY	OUR	US	ME	IT	THEIR	
THEM	HER	ITS	YOU	YOUR	OUR	

B Dis en anglais.

pour eux : ....
avec elle : ....
dans notre école : ....
son artiste préféré (à lui) :
....

pour nous : ....
avec elles : ....
avec leurs enfants : ....
son artiste préféré (à elle) :
....

C Complète les phrases suivantes avec les adjectifs possessifs ou pronoms personnels appropriés.

1. Canadians are very proud of .... flag.
2. First, we're going to talk about .... trip to Quebec. Then you can ask .... questions.
3. When did Canada celebrate .... 100th anniversary?

D Entoure le mot qui convient.

1. We saw a big brown bear just in front of us / our. It was not far from our / us tent.
2. The guide didn't speak French but his / him wife was bilingual.
3. Tribes from Asia settled in North America and the Amerindians are its / their descendants.
4. When the English defeated the French, the French ceded Canada to their / them.

2. Entraîne-toi à poser des questions. ► Aide : mémento, n°13

■ Pose les questions dont les réponses sont les expressions entre crochets.

1. Yesterday I had to leave home [at 7.00].

   ....

2. [My Mum] woke me up.

   ....

3. I put on a warm jacket [because it was very cold].

   ....

4. It cost [more than 100 dollars].

   ....

UNIT 3

Basics

① People and things that shape Canada.

► pages 42-43

1. Listen. ► page 42

A Ecoute neuf définitions et complète les phrases avec le relatif que tu entends : ***which, who, whose, that*** **ou** ***Ø.***
Puis, à l'aide des photos dans ton manuel, réponds aux questions :
Who is it? What is it?

	relatif		Who is it? What is it?
1. It is a sport	....	the Canadians invented.	....
2. They are sculptures	....	are made from tree-trunks.	....
3. It is an animal	....	cousin is the wapiti.	....
4. It is a tree	....	you get syrup from.	....
5. They are people	....	live along the Arctic circle.	....
6. It is an animal	....	is hunted for its fur.	....
7. She is someone	....	face is on Canadian coins and banknotes.	....
8. They were European settlers	....	the English defeated in Quebec.	....
9. They were Europeans	....	settled in Nova Scotia.	....

B Relis les phrases ci-dessus puis complète le tableau suivant avec les antécédents des relatifs (= les mots placés juste avant les relatifs). **Note tes conclusions dans le** ***Remember.***

... who	... which	... that	... Ø	... whose
....	....	....	....	....

REMEMBER

• L'emploi de certains relatifs dépend de l'antécédent :
– ***who*** ne s'emploie que lorsque l'antécédent est humain ☐ non humain ☐.
Exemple : ....
– ***which*** ne s'emploie que lorsque l'antécédent est humain ☐ non humain ☐.
Exemple : ....
• Les autres relatifs s'emploient aussi bien lorsque l'antécédent est humain ou non humain :
– ***that*** peut s'employer à la place de *who* et de *which*.
Exemple : ....
– **Ø** ne s'emploie que lorsqu'il est sujet ☐ complément ☐ du verbe.
Exemple : ....
– ***whose*** s'emploie lorsqu'il est complément du nom qui le suit (en français, ce relatif se traduit le plus souvent par le relatif « dont »).
Exemple : ....
• Lorsque le verbe est suivi d'une ***préposition***, celle-ci est rejetée en fin de phrase et le relatif est généralement Ø.
Exemple : un arbre dont on tire du sirop = ...

2. Make comments. ► page 43

A Complète les phrases par les relatifs *who, which, that, Ø, whose.* Pour certaines phrases, deux relatifs sont possibles.

1. John, ... parents live in Quebec, speaks French and English.
2. The totem pole .... we saw was very colourful.
3. This is a photo of the caribou .... my little brother was afraid of.
4. The maple trees .... grow in this park are huge.
5. It is someone .... he plays ice-hockey with.

B Traduis en anglais.

1. une carte qui montre les territoires indiens

....

2. des gens dont les ancêtres sont arrivés au XVIIIe siècle

....

3. les gens que nous avons rencontrés, les endroits que nous avons visités

....

4. un candidat pour qui j'ai voté

....

3. The day when ... ► page 43

■ Complète les phrases suivantes avec des exemples personnels puis traduis-les.

1. I'll always remember the day ....

....

2. Do you regret the time ....

....

3. I don't remember the place ....

....

Oral practice

► page 43

REMEMBER

Les finales en *-ian*, comme celles en *-ic* (unité 1) ou en *-ion* (unité 2), entraînent un accent sur la syllabe qui précède.

Exemples : ....

Cela peut entraîner un changement d'accentuation par rapport au mot de base.

Exemples : ....

■ D'après les règles d'accentuation que tu as vues dans les unités 1, 2 et 3, tu sais repérer les syllabes accentuées dans les mots suivants. Souligne-les et entraîne-toi à les lire.

ASIAN POPULATION MAGIC TRANSPORTATION HISTORIC
PHYSICIAN TRADITION ELECTRICIAN RUSSIAN COMPLETION

Listening

1. Listening comprehension. ► page 57

A

1. What Sarah says about her trip:
   - ".."
   - ".."
   - ".."

   She is sad ☐ disappointed ☐ enthusiastic ☐ furious ☐.

2. Nicole is Sarah's ....
   Jack met Nicole. • When? ....
   • Where? ....

   He liked her. ☐ He didn't like her. ☐

3. Mark is Sarah's dad ☐ friend ☐ brother ☐.
   Sarah drove Mark's snowmobile ☐ her dad's snowmobile ☐
   Nicole's snowmobile ☐.

B

4. Jim is Nicole's ....

5. Sarah took a photo of a snowmobile. Yes ☐ No ☐
   Why or why not? ....

6. Sarah mentions • a place: ....
   • a thing: ....
   • an animal: ....

C

7. Jack asks a question about ....
8. Sarah thinks his question is interesting ☐ annoying ☐.
9. Sarah is happy ☐ sorry ☐ disappointed ☐ because Jack is ....
   ....

D **Dictation.**

1. ....
2. ....
3. ....
4. ....
5. ....

2. Summary.

....
....
....
....
....
....
....

Basics

② Canada makes me dream. ► pages 44-45

1. Look and comment. ► page 44

A Lis ce que Cathy, jeune fille au pair, écrit à ses parents et souligne les verbes *let* et *make* ainsi que les verbes qui les suivent.

They make me do lots of things in the house: cook, water the plants, hoover.
But, they often go out and then they let me invite friends home; they also let me use their computer, their stereo, their camcorder … And, the little girl is very funny!
She makes me laugh a lot !

REMEMBER

• ***let*** exprime une autorisation ☐ une contrainte ☐ un effet produit ☐.
Exemple : ……………………………………………………………………………

make exprime une autorisation ☐ une contrainte ☐ un effet produit ☐.
Exemples : ……………………………………………………………………………
……………………………………………………………………………

• Ces deux verbes sont d'abord suivis d'un nom ou d'un pronom complément puis d'un autre verbe.

Sous quelle forme est le second verbe ? base verbale ☐ *to* + base verbale ☐

B Utilise le verbe *make* pour construire des phrases comme dans l'exemple suivant :

The students stood up.
→ The teacher made them stand up.

1. The taxi driver stopped immediately.
→ The policeman ……………………………………………………………
2. I opened my suitcase.
→ The customs officer ……………………………………………………………
3. We cried when we saw the film.
→ This sad story ……………………………………………………………
4. The gangsters ran away.
→ The alarm ……………………………………………………………

C Termine les phrases suivantes en utilisant le verbe *let* à la forme affirmative ou négative suivi d'un pronom complément et du verbe entre crochets.

1. Our teacher was so furious that he ……………………………… during the break. [go out]
2. My mum says that when I am 18, she ……………………………… her car. [drive]
3. My sister is selfish; she ……………………………… her computer. [use]
4. The players were exhausted. So, their coach ……………………………… for quite a long time. [have a pause]

2. Listen. ▶ page 44

■ Ecoute une fille et un garçon parler de leur école. Chacun dit à tour de rôle :
- ce qu'on les laisse faire ;
- ce qu'on ne les laisse pas faire ;
- ce qu'on les oblige à faire.

Coche les cases équivalentes.

	They are allowed to …	They are not allowed to …	They have to …
1. … wear what they want			
2. … wear what they want			
3. … work with a partner			
4. … work with a partner			
5. … leave school when a teacher is absent			
6. … leave school when a teacher is absent			
7. … tidy up their classrooms			
8. … tidy up their classrooms			

3. What makes you laugh? ▶ page 45

■ Dis en anglais.

1. Qu'est ce qui te fait rire ?

……………………………………………………………………………………

2. Cela m'endort.

……………………………………………………………………………………

3. Pourquoi l'as-tu fait pleurer ?

……………………………………………………………………………………

4. Reported speech. ▶ page 45

A Lis les phrases suivantes. Dans quelles phrases sont mentionnées les personnes auxquelles Adrian s'adresse ? Entoure-les puis complète le tableau *Remember*.

a. Adrian says, "Go to bed!"
b. He tells the campers to go to bed.
c. He says, "Don't stay up late!"
d. He tells them not to stay up late.

REMEMBER

• Au style direct « dire » se traduit par le verbe ………………

Exemple : ……………………………………………………………………

• Lorsque l'on rapporte (style indirect) un ordre donné à quelqu'un, « dire » se traduit par le verbe …………………

Lorsque cet ordre est négatif, on emploie : ………… + complément d'attribution + …………………………

Exemple : ……………………………………………………………………

B Complète ces phrases avec le verbe *tell* ou le verbe *say*.

1. Parents and teachers constantly .... us .... work harder.
2. What do your parents .... when you come home late?
3. My mother always .... my little brother .... eat with his fingers.
4. How many times a day do you .... "thank you"?
5. Last night, I .... my brother .... annoy me and .... leave me alone because I was studying for my test in English.

Oral practice

► page 45

REMEMBER
Certaines consonnes finales d'un mot ne s'entendent pas : elles sont « absorbées » par la consonne du mot suivant lorsqu'elles sont identiques.
Exemples : ....
Cela peut être le cas avec la terminaison *-ed* d'un verbe.
Exemple : ....

Dans les phrases suivantes, raye les consonnes finales qui disparaissent à l'oral.

1. I won't take my coat. I'll leave it here.
2. He has seen several wild animals.
3. They rented a big black car.
4. You should stop paddling.
5. He asked two questions.

Listening

1. Listening comprehension. ► page 45

A What does the sign say?

NO BEARS IN THE AREA	BEARS! GO AWAY!	DO NOT FEED THE BEARS
a. ☐	b. ☐	c. ☐

B

1. If you see a bear, • you must ....
   • you mustn't ....
2. Carla doesn't want to ....
3. She wants to ....

C

4. First, Dave sees some .... which are
- ☐ not very big.
- ☐ enormous.
- ☐ very small.

5. Then he sees ....

6. So, Carla and Dave feel
- ☐ frightened.
- ☐ upset.
- ☐ excited.

D

	TRUE	FALSE
7. Carla wants to take a picture.	☐	☐
8. Dave thinks Carla must keep quiet.	☐	☐
9. Dave thinks bears don't mind photographers.	☐	☐

E

	Dave thinks …	Carla thinks …	
10			… the other one is not speaking seriously.
11			… for bears, guns and cameras are the same.
12			… bears are clever.

F

13. .... sees Carla and Dave.
14. .... wants to leave.
15. .... wants to stay.
16. Last year, a bear attacked ....
17. .... goes first.
18. .... panics.

G **Report what they say.**

1. Dave tells Carla to ....
2. Dave tells Carla to ....
3. Dave asks Carla ....
4. Carla tells Dave ....

2. Summary.

....
....
....
....
....
....
....

3 The Inuit used to be called "Eskimos".

► page 46

1 What did the Inuit use to do?

A Prononciation de *used to / didn't use to*

REMEMBER

• Dans l'expression ***used to***, la marque *-ed* du prétérit ne s'entend pas. Pourquoi ?

....

• L'expression ***used to / didn't use to*** se prononce avec le son [s].
Ecoute et répète : *They used to be called "Eskimos".* *They didn't use to have cars.*

• Le verbe ***use*** (utiliser) se prononce avec le son [z].
Ecoute et répète : *They use a floatplane.* *They used to use kayaks.*

B Ecris le son [s] ou le son [z] à côté de chaque verbe souligné.

1. I used [.....] to be very shy. Fortunately, I'm not any more.
2. My brother always uses [.....] my hairbrush, and it makes me mad.
3. It didn't use [.....] to rain so much.
4. What shampoo do you use [.....]?

C Lis les phrases suivantes.

a. *The Inuit **used to sleep** in igloos. Now they sleep in houses.*
b. *Joe **slept** in an igloo when he got lost in the Far North.*

Quelle phrase évoque quelque chose qui ne s'est passé qu'une fois ? **a.** ☐ **b.** ☐
Laquelle évoque quelque chose qui était courant autrefois ? **a.** ☐ **b.** ☐
Pourquoi ne puis-je pas dire : *In Canada, it used to be very cold in winter?*

....

D *not ... any more.*
Observe ces phrases :

a. *I used to be very sporty.* **b.** *I am not very sporty any more.*
c. *I used to go canoeing.* **d.** *I don't go canoeing any more.*

• Les phrases **a** et **c** évoquent :
le passé ☐ le présent ☐, comme l'indique l'expression: ....

• Les phrases **b** et **d** évoquent :
le passé ☐ le présent ☐ , comme l'indiquent les auxiliaires ....

• *I don't go canoeing any more* signifie : Je ne fais pas de canoë. ☐
Je ne fais plus de canoë. ☐
Je ne fais jamais de canoë. ☐

UNIT 3

E Transforme les phrases ci-dessous, comme dans l'exemple donné.

We used to live close to nature.
→ We ***don't*** *live close to it* ***any more****.*

1. Our canoes used to be made of wood.
→ ....
2. We used to go hunting very often.
→ ....
3. There used to be many caribous in this forest.
→ ....
4. We used to have many dogs to feed.
→ ....
5. Women used to make all the clothes.
→ ....

2. What didn't the Inuit use to do?

A Lis les phrases suivantes.

The Inuit ***used to hunt*** *with arrows. They* ***didn't use to hunt*** *with rifles.*
Did *Inuit children* ***use to hunt*** *too?*

Quel verbe porte la marque du prétérit? *use* ☐ *hunt* ☐

REMEMBER
Lorsque je veux évoquer des situations qui existaient autrefois et qui n'existent plus aujourd'hui, j'utilise .... suivi de *to* puis du verbe indiquant l'action ou la situation. Ce second verbe n'est pas conjugué.
Exemple : *When I was a kid, I* .... *to* ....

B Complète les phrases suivantes avec *used to* ou *didn't use to* suivi d'un verbe approprié.

1. ... you .... with a teddy bear when you were a baby?
2. When my grandmother was a child, there .... any computers in her home.
3. And she .... to school on Saturday mornings.
4. In the 19th century, many children .... to in factories.

C Dis en anglais :

1. Est-ce que tu écoutais du reggae, autrefois ?
....
2. Autrefois, il y avait un cinéma dans cette rue.
....
3. Avant, je n'aimais pas la nourriture épicée.
....

More Words

► page 47

1. A word puzzle.

In the grid, find ten words from the list and three animals we can see in Canada.
(Words can be read from left to right, right to left, upward or backward, and crosswise.)

H	T	S	E	I	C	E	P	S	D
N	W	I	L	D	L	I	F	E	R
C	W	H	X	N	Y	L	R	F	E
E	L	Y	A	S	N	E	S	T	H
A	B	A	R	L	G	X	B	S	T
G	V	U	W	N	E	T	E	A	A
L	W	P	A	D	R	I	A	L	E
E	I	D	L	C	A	N	V	I	F
O	N	M	K	I	E	C	E	A	G
E	G	K	A	E	B	T	R	T	R

Words from the list.
1. ....
2. ....
3. ....
4. ....
5. ....
6. ....
7. ....
8. ....
9. ....
10. ....

Animals.
1. ....
2. ....
3. ....

2. A holiday in Italy.

Complete the following text with the words from the list on page 47.

Mr and Mrs Wilson are going on a package tour in Italy. They are looking at what is planned for them.

Mr Wilson: So, we arrive in Rome on Thursday evening. On Friday, they take us on a .... of the city by bus. Then, we visit a .... where recent archaeological finds are exhibited.

Mrs Wilson: And after lunch?

Mr Wilson: The afternoon is free and we can go .... on our own.

Mrs Wilson: Aren't we going to any .... ? I'd like to see some Italian paintings.

Mr Wilson: Yes, on Saturday.

Mrs Wilson: Don't you think the children will be bored?

Mr Wilson: Well, on Sunday we go to a .... They'll be able to swim and play on the beach there.

3. Coin New Words.

A Complete the grid. Be careful with the spelling of the suffix *-ful* (only one *l*).

noun	adjective *-ful*	adjective *-less*
pain *(douleur)*	painful *(douloureux)*	painless *(indolore)*
power *(puissance)*	.... (..............................)	.... (..........................)
use *(utilité)*	.... (..............................)	.... (..........................)
harm *(mal)*	.... *(nuisible)*	.... *(inoffensif)*

B Using the box, find the English for :

- gracieux : ....
- paisible : ....
- édenté : ....
- immobile : ....
- effrayant: ....

- *peace*
- *motion* (mouvement)
- *fright* (peur)
- *grace*
- *tooth*

Topic

A family trip across Canada
► pages 48-49

1. Comprehension.
► page 48

A General comprehension.

1. Who is the narrator? Gary ☐ Rachel ☐ Gary's parents ☐
2. The route they followed was:
   - the west coast → Nunavut → the east coast ☐
   - the east coast → Northern Territories → the west coast ☐
   - the west coast → Northern Territories → the east coast ☐

B *Vancouver*: Quote the text to justify the following sentences.

1. Gary is fourteen.

....

2. His parents think he won't spend his holidays with them at the age of sixteen.

....

3. Gary's mother isn't a teacher any more.

....

4. Rachel thinks her parents have found a good plan to make Gary stop playing computer games.

....

5. Rachel will have to tolerate Gary sitting next to her in the car throughout their long journey.

....

6. And she isn't enthusiastic about it!

....

C *Yellowknife*: Put the following sentences in the right order.

a. They kept watching the lynx as long as they could.
b. The moose noticed their presence and looked quietly at them.
c. There were birds of prey in the area.
d. The lynx didn't move when it saw them.
e. They stopped paddling to watch the lynx longer.
f. They couldn't see the grizzly very distinctly because it was too far away.

1.	2.	3.	4.	5.	6.
b					

D ***Bay of Fundy*: Complete the following sentences.**

1. Gary's parents make him: ....
....
....
2. .... used to live in Grand Pré.
3. .... attacked them.
4. Friends and families were separated because ....
5. This happened in ...., ... ago.
6. Rachel got really angry; she .... and she...
7. On July the 31st they will ....

2. Find the English for:

• pendant leurs vacances d'été :	• toute la journée : ....
• toute notre famille :	• ils nous ont regardés fixement : ....
• dans deux ans :	• au loin : ....
• cela sera amusant :	• au moins : ....
• tout l'été :	• avoir lieu : ....
• supporter son frère :	• se mettre en colère : ....
• le siège arrière :	• éparpiller : ....
• tôt le matin :	• crier : ....

3. Linking word. ► page 49

*We woke up early in the morning **so that** we could enjoy the nice weather all day long.*

A **Match each linking word with its translation.**

whereas •	• *de sorte que, pour que*
and yet •	• *alors que*
so that •	• *et pourtant*

B **Complete the following sentences with *so that, whereas* or *and yet.***

1. Gary thought his Mum wanted to take him on a trip across Canada .... he could know more about his own country.
2. Rachel was upset by the story of the French-speaking Acadians .... Gary didn't seem to mind.
3. Rachel said, "How exciting!" with a smile .... she didn't like the idea of sitting next to her brother in the back seat of the car for 6,000 km.
4. The moose were not very excited to see Gary's family .... Gary was very pleased to see them.
5. Gary's parents took their children to the Bay of Fundy .... they could see whales.

4. Reading aloud.

■ Get ready to read this part of the text aloud.

> *"This is a plot so that Gary won't spend all summer inside playing computer games, isn't it?", said my younger sister, Rachel. She is ten, she thinks she knows everything and she wants to know everything.*

5. Writing task. ► page 49

> *Something made you furious / sad / happy today.*
> *Write a page in an imaginary diary.*

Quelques conseils.

1. Choisis d'abord quel sentiment tu vas exprimer dans ton journal et ce qui peut avoir déclenché ce sentiment :

- ***furious:*** *a bad mark / lots of work / something unfair / you lost or forgot or broke something / someone said or did something to you / ...*
- ***sad:*** *a quarrel / bad news / trouble in the family / something happened to someone you love / ...*
- ***happy:*** *a present / a visit / good news / ...*

2. Explique ce qui a provoqué ta réaction. Pour cela, raconte l'histoire.
Dis :

- **où** cela s'est passé :
  at school / at home / at a friend's house / in a public place / ...
- **qui** sont les personnes impliquées :
  a friend / a teacher / someone in your family / a girlfriend or a boyfriend / ...
- **quand** cela s'est passé :
  this morning / last week / at ... / during ... / while (+ be -ing) / before or after / ...
- **ce qui s'est passé** (prétérit simple / prétérit en *be + -ing*)

N'oublie pas **les mots de liaison (*and, but, then, so that, and yet, actually, whereas*)**.

3. Termine par une ou deux phrases de **conclusion** : tu peux tirer une « morale » de l'histoire, exprimer une opinion générale, prendre une décision, etc ...

More about...

... nature and culture in Canada ▶ pages 50-51

1. General comprehension.

■ Complete the two grids below.

What to see in nature	Where	When
....	....	....
....	....	....
....	....	....

City	Province	Main tourist attraction	Languages (other than English)
....	*Quebec*	....	....
Toronto	....	....	....
....	*Alberta*	....	
....	....	*sea and mountain*	....

2. Detailed comprehension.

A Rewrite the following sentences after correcting the mistakes.

1. Orcas are the largest kind of whales.

   ....

2. Whales come to Quebec to give birth to their babies.

   ....

3. You can see beluga whales only in the summer.

   ....

4. Polar bears leave the Hudson Bay area when it gets cold.

   ....

5. Polar bears avoid contact with humans.

   ....

6. You needn't be afraid of polar bears.

   ....

B Complete the following sentences.

1. People can do their shopping without getting cold in ....
2. In Vancouver, people can go to the beach on the..
3. In Edmonton, people can go to the beach in the ....
4. 2/3 of the population speak .... in ....
5. 1/3 of the population is .... in ....

C Cross out what we can't do in *Edmonton Shopping Mall.*

- slide down a toboggan
- play mini-golf
- go skiing
- swim
- watch a film
- ride a scooter
- play baseball
- go whale-watching
- ride a horse
- go skating
- eat out
- spend money

D What is it?

1. You can eat it when you haven't got much time to cook. ....
2. It's the quickest way to fasten a jacket or jeans. ....
3. You can have fun and learn at the same time when you play it. ....
4. It can save people's lives. ....

E Who are they?

1. .... was born in British Columbia.
2. .... became an actor in Ontario.
3. .... began working for the Canadian television.
4. .... started acting in the largest city in Canada.

QUIZ

► pages 54-55

How much do you know about the cinema?

1 The first cinema in the world opened:

in London ☐

in Paris ☐

in Hollywood ☐

2 Match each name with an "invention":

(1) Georges Mélies

(2) The Lumière Brothers

(3) Thomas Edison

• the invention of the kinetoscope:

(a) ☐ (b) ☐ (c) ☐

• the invention of the *cinématographe*:

(a) ☐ (b) ☐ (c) ☐

• the telling of stories in films:

(a) ☐ (b) ☐ (c) ☐

3 Who was the first to introduce special effects?

an American ☐

an Englishman ☐

a Frenchman ☐

4 Most silent films were:

very long ☐ very short ☐

5 Cross the odd man out:

• live actors improvising dialogues
• piano playing
• silent films
• Technicolor

6 "Talkies" appeared :

in the 1900s ☐

in the early 1920s ☐

in the late 1920s ☐

7 Film producers left for Hollywood:

because of the weather and the landscapes ☐

because of bigger movie theaters ☐

because of the clean air ☐

8 The French translation of *Gone with the Wind* is:

Partis au gré du vent ☐

Autant en emporte le vent ☐

9 Match each film with a date.

(a) Apocalypse Now •	• 1939
(b) The Jazz Singer •	• 1978
(c) Shrek •	• 1927
(d) Grease •	• 1979
(e) Gone with the Wind •	• 2001

10 Which of those films mentioned above is:

• a musical (*comédie musicale*)

(d) ☐ (e) ☐

• a love story taking place during the Civil War

(d) ☐ (e) ☐

• a war film

(a) ☐ (c) ☐

11 Put these elements in chronological order (number them from 1 to 6):

... the use of computers

... the *cinématographe*

... the introduction of sound

... the kinetoscope

... the introduction of colour

... the first special effects

Un peu de rattrapage

1. Les formes de *be*. ►Aide : mémento n°15 et n°18

A Complète les phrases avec *be* au présent, au prétérit, au *present perfect* ou avec *will*.

1. Where .... you born?
2. How old .... you .... in 2020?
3. How many Black slaves .... there in the United States in 1865?
4. She .... never .... so disappointed!
5. There .... so much traffic that we missed our plane.
6. Next week I .... absent for two days.

2. Les participes passés. ►Aide : verbes irréguliers p.188-190

■ Retrouve huit participes passés (p.p.) et écris-les, ainsi que leur base verbale. (b.v.).

	WOHNS	WOLNB	DNEHDI	VINGE
pp :	....	....	....	....
bv :	....	....	....	....

	DOTL	AKTNE	TUC	ENOD
pp :	....	....	....	....
bv :	....	....	....	....

3. Entraîne-toi à poser des questions. ► Aide : mémento, n°12 et n°13

■ Pose les questions dont les réponses sont les expressions entre crochets.

1. In the United States there were [10,000] cinemas in the 1900s.
....

2. Producers left for California [because there are varied landscapes and constant sunlight].
....

3. Most silent films lasted [only a few minutes].
....

4. [Georges Mélies] introduced special effects in films.
....

5. Alfred Hitchcock directed [more than fifty] films.
....

Basics

① A story that was adapted for the screen.

▶ pages 56-57

1. Tell the story. ▶ page 56

A Formation de la voix passive.

*Many novels **are adapted** for the screen.*
*The adaptation of the "Addams Family" **was directed by** Barry Sonnenfeld.*
*The scenes **were shot** in a studio.*

Ces phrases sont à la voix passive.
• Quelles sont leurs différents auxiliaires ? ....
• Ce sont les formes du verbe ....
Les mots *adapted, directed, shot* sont des verbes au ....

REMEMBER
• La voix passive se forme, comme en français, à l'aide de l'auxiliaire .... suivi d'un verbe au ....
• L'agent (= celui qui fait l'action) est introduit par la préposition ......
• Exemple : ....

B Voici six phrases sur la *Famille Addams.* Coche la réponse qui te semble juste.

	1.	2.	3.	4.	5.	6.
a.						
b.						

C Complète ces phrases en mettant le verbe à la voix passive au présent ou au prétérit.

1. During Hollywood's Golden Age, the producers .... by California's sunlight. [attract]
2. When sound .... , some silent film stars didn't survive the transition. [introduce]
3. Some film stars .... [very well pay]
4. Some special effects .... by easy tricks (*trucages*). [produce]
5. The technique of morphing .... first .... in 1990. [use]

D Voix passive ou voix active ?

Thing opened the door.
L'élément mis en relief est celui qui fait l'action : la phrase est à la voix ....

The door was opened by Thing.
L'élément mis en relief est celui qui « subit » l'action : la phrase est à la voix ....

Construis des phrases au présent à la voix active ou à la voix passive avec les verbes proposés. Le sujet grammatical de chaque phrase est l'élément mis en relief par une flèche. Ne mentionne pas le complément d'agent.

• give • shoot • hide • arrest • take pictures • award

1. ....
2. ....
3. ....
4. ....
5. ....
6. ....

2. What must be done? ► page 57

A Ecoute six phrases et écris la forme de l'auxiliaire *be* que tu entends.

1. .... seen **2.** .... shot **3.** .... ordered
4. .... ordered **5.** .... sent **6.** .... made

B Complète les phrases suivantes avec l'une des formes de l'auxiliaire *be* de l'exercice précédent.

1. You know what! A film .... shot in our school next month.
2. Tell me: who .... interviewed? I don't recognize this voice.
3. This exercise is short. It .... done in a few minutes.
4. There used to be a statue here, but it .... removed.
5. The past and past participle of irregular verbs .... learned by heart.

3. Reported speech. ▶ page 57

A **Observe ces phrases :**

*"I'**m** crazy about musicals. I **love** that type of films."*
*Kate **says** that she **is** crazy about musicals, and that she **loves** that type of films.*
*Kate **said** that she **was** crazy about musicals, and that she **loved** that type of films.*

REMEMBER

style direct	style indirect
Présent	**verbe introducteur au présent** → **paroles rapportées au présent** *(**says**, answers, asks ...)*
*"I'**m** crazy about musicals."*	She .... that she .... crazy about musicals.
*"I **love** that type of films."*	She .... that she .... that type of films.
Présent	**verbe introducteur au prétérit** → **paroles rapportées au prétérit** *(**said**, answered, asked ...)*
*"I'**m** crazy about musicals."*	She .... that she .... crazy about musicals.
*"I **love** that type of films."*	She .... that she .... that type of films.

B **Réécris le dialogue d'origine entre Alice et sa mère à partir de ce commentaire.**

Alice told her mother that she couldn't stay for dinner. Her mother asked her where she was going. Alice explained that a boy in her class had free tickets for Spielberg's latest film and it was something she did not want to miss. Her mother wanted to know who she was going with. Alice said that she was going with two other students. Her mother asked her what time she was coming back home. Alice answered that she had no idea.

1. Alice : ".."
2. Her mother : ".. ?"
3. Alice : "..
...."
4. Her mother : ".. ?"
5. Alice : ".."
6. Her mother : ".. ?"
7. Alice : ".."

Oral practice

► page 57

A Souligne les syllabes accentuées.

DIRECT → DIRECTOR COMPOSE → COMPOSER

REMEMBER
Les terminaisons *-er* / *-or* entraînent ☐ n'entraînent pas ☐ de modification de l'accentuation par rapport au mot de base. Elles ne sont jamais accentuées.
Exemple : ....

B D'après les règles d'accentuation que tu as apprises dans les unités précédentes et celle-ci, entraîne-toi à lire les mots de la liste ci-dessous, après avoir souligné les syllabes accentuées :

MONSTER TRAFFIC MOTHER LATER HORROR MANSION

MEMBER ANCESTOR COMIC PROJECTOR INTERVENTION

Listening

1. Listening comprehension. ► page 57

A

1. Match the elements in the two columns:

science fiction •	• *African Skies*
a love story •	• *Stardust*
Sam Scott •	• *The Beginners*

2. Chris saw ☐ didn't see ☐ the film and he liked it ☐ didn't like it ☐.

3. Chris has ☐ hasn't ☐ read the book and he liked it ☐ didn't like it ☐.

4. Julia has ☐ hasn't ☐ read the book.

B

5. They compare the book with the film.

The story is the same ☐ different ☐.

The scene with monkeys is in the book only ☐.
in the film only ☐.
in both the book and the film ☐.

6. Julia was disappointed ☐ amazed ☐ by the scene.

7. In the film, lots of the best scenes ....
and many scenes ....

C

8. Chris is surprised because Julia said
that she ....
and that she ....

D

9. Who likes Sam Scott? Chris ☐ Julia ☐ both of them ☐

10. Julia asks Chris if ....

11. Chris answers ....

E Report what Julia said.

1. Julia said that ....

2. She said that ....

3. She said that ....

2. Summary.

....
....
....
....
....
....
....

2 When a secretary is asked to put money in a safe ... ► pages 58-59

1. Comment. ► page 58

■ **Peux-tu compléter cette courte introduction présentant *Psycho*?**

Hitchcock .... Psycho in 1960. It .... in white and black, and the .... was played by Anthony Perkins.
The film was soon .... as a ....
in thrillers and *Psycho* became one ....

2. Listen. ► page 58

■ **Complète le début de l'histoire avec les formes verbales que tu entends.**

Marion, a young secretary, ... the money she ....
to put in a safe (*coffre-fort*) and .... town in her car.
She .... for the night at a motel. She .... by the owner, Norman Bates, who .... in a strange house nearby. Marion .... and .... him talking to his old mother.

3. Continue the story. ► page 58

A Lis les phrases à la voix active dans lesquelles le verbe est suivi de deux compléments. Puis observe ces mêmes phrases à la voix passive.

Voix active	Voix passive
Mary gave <u>me</u> (1) <u>a present</u> (2).	I was given a present.
They asked <u>John</u> (1) <u>his new address</u> (2).	John was asked his new address.
Someone showed <u>him</u> (1) <u>the way</u> (2).	He was shown the way.

Tu peux remarquer que, dans les phrases à la voix passive :
le complément 1 est devenu sujet ☐ est resté complément ☐ ;
le complément 2 est devenu sujet ☐ est resté complément ☐ .

Complète la traduction :
I was given a present : On .... un cadeau.
He was shown the way : .... le chemin.

Remarques :

• On peut trouver cette construction avec d'autres verbes tels que *tell, offer, send, expect, teach.*

• Elle permet d'insister sur **la personne** à qui l'on demande, montre, donne, etc … plus que sur la chose demandée, montrée, donnée, etc. Souvent le complément d'agent n'est pas mentionné.

REMEMBER

Avec les verbes suivis de deux compléments, tels que *ask* , ……………… , ……………… , ……………… , ……………… , …………… , …………… , ……………… , si l'on passe de la voix active à la voix passive – donc si l'on change de point de vue – le complément d'attribution peut devenir ………….. de la phrase au passif.

Cette construction n'a pas son équivalent en français : on utilise alors la tournure avec ………………

Exemple : ………………………… → ……………………………………

B Mets les phrases à la voix passive en respectant les temps et en prenant comme sujet les mots en italiques. (Ne pas mentionner l'agent.)

1. The fans expect *Manchester United* to win the match.
……………………………………………………………………………………
2. Someone will tell *you* the whole story later.
……………………………………………………………………………………
3. The manager offered *my mother* a more interesting job.
……………………………………………………………………………………
4. And he will give *her* a higher salary.
……………………………………………………………………………………
5. Fans often ask *celebrities* for pictures with autographs.
……………………………………………………………………………………

Oral practice

► page 59

Ecoute six phrases et coche les bonnes réponses.

1. given ☐	giving ☐		**2.** given ☐	giving ☐	
3. taken ☐	taking ☐		**4.** taken ☐	taking ☐	
5. eaten ☐	eating ☐		**6.** eaten ☐	eating ☐	

 ► page 59

1. Listening comprehension.

A

1. Jimmy is going to act in a film.   Yes ☐   No ☐
2. Miranda thinks he is   serious ☐   not serious ☐ .
3. The film was mentioned   on the radio ☐   on TV ☐   in the press ☐ .

B

4. What did Jimmy do?

a. ☐

b. ☐

c. ☐

5. Jimmy asked questions ☐ .   Someone asked him questions ☐ .
6. He .... for an audition.

C

7. Jimmy was auditioned by the film director.   Yes ☐   No ☐
8. He had to improvise a scene.   Yes ☐   No ☐

D

9. How much money will Jimmy get? ....
10. Jimmy   has read ☐   hasn't read ☐   the script.
11. What happens in the film?

a. ☐

b. ☐

c. ☐

12. Jimmy's part   is ☐   isn't ☐   important because he plays the part of ....

E Dictation.

1. ....
2. ....
3. ....

2. Summary.

....

....

....

....

....

....

....

Basics

UNIT 4

3 Special effects are created by using a bagful of tricks. ► page 60

1. What does it sound like ?

■ Ecoute six bruits et coche la réponse qui te semble juste.

	1.	2.	3.	4.	5.	6.
a.						
b.						

2. What does it look like?

A **Lis cet extrait de scénario et souligne les verbes *look, look like, sound et sound like* :**

In a parking lot, a young lady is waiting. She looks nervous.
A man comes up to her. He looks like an extraterrestrial. When he says hello to her, his voice sounds like a robot's. She answers but she sounds terrified.

Le mot qui suit ***sound*** et ***look*** est	un adjectif ☐	un nom ☐.
Le mot qui suit ***sound like*** et ***look like*** est	un adjectif ☐	un nom ☐.
like est alors	un verbe ☐	une préposition ☐.

Les verbes *smell, taste, feel* peuvent aussi se construire avec la préposition *like* :

*It **smells** good / awful!* → Ça sent bon / mauvais!
*It **smells like** coffee.* → Ça sent le café. (= on dirait du café)
*This water **tastes** funny.* → Cette eau a un goût bizarre.
*This chewing gum **tastes like** lemon.* → Ce chewing gum a un goût de citron. (= on dirait du citron)
*This material **feels** soft.* → Ce tissu est doux (au toucher).
*This material **feels like** silk.* → Ce tissu ressemble à de la soie. (= au toucher, on dirait de la soie.)

REMEMBER

Pour parler d'une sensation (quelque chose que l'on perçoit par l'un des cinq sens), on peut la décrire ou bien la comparer avec autre chose.

sensation liée :	description	comparaison
• à la vue :	*look* + adjectif	*look* + *like* + nom
• à l'ouïe :	.... + adjectif	.... +.............. + nom
• à l'odorat :	.... + adjectif	.... +.............. + nom
• au toucher :	.... + adjectif	.... +.............. + nom
• au goût :	.... + adjectif	.... +.............. + nom

B Complète les phrases suivantes en utilisant les verbes *look , sound, smell, feel, taste* suivis ou non de la préposition *like*.

1. Dave, this is the best song you've ever sung! It .... beautiful! You really .... a professional singer.
2. Phil – Hello, John! This is Phil!
John – Phil! You .... your father; you've got exactly the same voice!
3. Teacher – Mary, you .... discouraged. Well, the test is a bit long and .... difficult, but it isn't.
4. Colin – See you next Saturday at the party.
Steve – That .... great!
5. What's the matter? You .... terrible! You.......................... a zombie!
6. The pizza is delicious. It .... the ones we had in Italy.
7. Something .... good in the kitchen. What are you cooking?
8. This sweater .... so soft , it .... silk!

3. How are these effects created?

A Observe les deux phrases suivantes :

(1a) *I'm fed up **with homework**.* **(1b)** *I'm fed up **with working** all the time.*
(2a) *I'm interested **in music**.* **(2b)** *I'm interested in going to that concert.*

Dans les phrases **1a** et **2a**, ***with*** et ***in*** sont suivis d'un nom ☐ d'un verbe ☐ .
Dans les phrases **1b** et **2b**, ***with*** et ***in*** sont suivis d'un nom ☐ d'un verbe ☐ .

A quelle forme sont les verbes qui suivent ***with*** et ***in*** ? ....

Les mots *with, without, after, before, of, by, for* et *in* sont des adverbes ☐
des prépositions ☐.

REMEMBER
Tout verbe qui suit une préposition est au gérondif.
Exemples : • ....
• ....

B Complète les phrases suivantes en utilisant une des prépositions de la liste et l'expression donnée entre parenthèses à la bonne forme.

• *after* • *before* • *by* • *instead of* (au lieu de) • *without*

1. People should always wash their hands .... [eat]
2. They should never drive .... [drink alcohol]
3. They should never ride a motorbike .... [wear a helmet]
4. They should practise sport .... [watch matches on TV]
5. They could keep fit .... [get more exercise]
6. They should cook healthy meals .... [buy fast food]

More Words

page 61

1. Hidden words.

■ Find six words from the list.

1. ROCKSTAUND ....
2. TROUBBLESCK ....
3. ARCHTRACE ....
4. CORTIRED ....
5. TITBLUES ....
6. CREAMEPITES ....

2. The making of a film.

■ Complete the sentences with some of the words from the list.

1. The names of everyone who participated in the making of a film appear in the .... at the end of the film.
2. When films are .... we don't hear the real voices of the actors.
3. When foreign films are not dubbed there are ....
4. Actors have to learn their .... by heart.
5. In the credits the names of the .... are followed by the names of the actors who played them.
6. Everyone who acted in a film is part of the ....

3. Coin New Words.

A Adverbs, adjectives and nouns.

• Now you now how some adverbs (*-ly*), some adjectives (*-less, -ful*), some nouns (*-ness*) are created. Put the following words in the right box.

• *thankful* • *hugely* • *friendless* • *needless* • *freshness* • *admittedly* • *cheerful* • *rudeness* • *short-sightedness* • *smoothly* • *sickness*

adverbs	adjectives	nouns
....	....	....
....	....	....
....	....	....
	....	....

• Which noun means:

la myopie : .... la fraîcheur : ....
l'insolence : .... la maladie : ....

B What's the English for:

l'obscurité : .... (adjective: *dark*)
le bonheur : .... (adjective: *happy*)
l'égoïsme : .... (adjective: *selfish*)
la paresse : .... (adjective: *lazy*)
la solitude : .... (adjective: *lonely*)

"Care" = *le soin.*

soigneux : .... (noun: *care*)
négligent : ....
soigneusement : ....
négligemment : ....
la négligence : ....

▶ pages 62-63

What is it like to be a film star?

1. Comprehension. ▶ page 62

A Kate Winslet: Rewrite the sentences below next to the headings (= *titres*).

- They suggested that Kate was refused roles because she didn't look like a Hollywood star.
- It made her a star.
- They sent her to a theatre school.
- She was rejected because she was overweight and not wealthy.
- You don't have to be supermodel-thin to be successful as an actor.
- She has always wanted to be an actress.
- She didn't want to be sucked into the crazy Hollywood machine.

Kate's one ambition in life: ....

Her parents' help: ....

The problems she had in school: ....

....

The effect of Titanic on her professional life:

a- the positive aspect: ....

b- what she wanted to avoid: ....

....

The reaction of the tabloid press: ....

....

Kate's opinion about physical appearance and success in films: ....

....

B Brad Pitt: Are these statements true (T) or false (F)? Justify your answer by quoting from the text.

1. Brad Pitt is considered as an extremely attractive person. T ☐ F ☐

....

....

2. Some people think that other actors are as sexy as he is. T ☐ F ☐

....

....

3. His fans are very curious about what he does, where he goes and what he says. T ☐ F ☐

....

....

4. A radio station encouraged his fans to respect his privacy. T ☐ F ☐

....

....

5. He thinks his private life is his own business. (= *ne regarde que lui*) T ☐ F ☐

....

....

6. He wants to protect his privacy. T ☐ F ☐

....

....

2. Find the English for:

• une école privée très chère :	• Il n'est pas étonnant que ... : ....
• trop gros :	• par exemple : ....
• aisé, riche :	• arriver à, parvenir à : ....
• se faire traiter de tous les noms :	• appartenir à : ....
• camarade de classe :	• faire face à, affronter : ....
• une idylle (histoire d'amour) :	• faire un procès à quelqu'un : ....

3. Linking word. ► page 63

Brad Pitt doesn't let photographers take pictures of his private life.
***As a result**, anyone who tries to invade his privacy is taken to court.*

A Match each linking word with its translation.

whereas •	• *de sorte que*
and yet •	• *en conséquence*
so that •	• *et pourtant*
as a result •	• *alors que*

B Complete the following sentences with *whereas, so that* or *As a result.*

1. Kate Winslet's parents sent her to a theatre school .... her dream came true.
2. She is not supermodel-thin .... some journalists said she was refused roles because of her physical appearance.
3. She thinks some people who are overweight can be very happy .... people who are thin may sometimes feel very unhappy.
4. Kate Winslet's was criticized by tabloids .... *People Magazine* gave Brad Pitt the title of "The Sexiest Man Alive".
5. Brad Pitt doesn't want people to know about him. .... he protects his privacy as much as he can.
6. Paparazzi try to take pictures of Brad Pitt's private life .... his fans can know everything about him.

4. Reading aloud. ► page 63

■ Get ready to read this part of the text aloud:

He is determined to control the effects of fame by protecting his privacy. He doesn't let photographers take pictures of his private life. As a result, anyone who tries to invade his privacy is taken to court.

5. Writing task. ► page 63

You have just been offered a part in a film and you want to accept it.
Your parents do not agree. Imagine the conversation between you and them.

Quelques conseils.

Tu peux annoncer le sujet par des considérations d'ordre général sur les relations parents / enfants (*agree / get on well / quarrel / understand / worry*).
Il s'agit d'une conversation. Il faut donc aller à la ligne à chaque changement de personnage et réécrire son nom.
Les deux premières répliques permettent de présenter la situation et les réactions de part et d'autre.

	YOU	YOUR PARENT/S
immediate reactions	*lucky / excited / enthusiastic / happy / delighted / proud*	*worried / upset / suspicious / panicked*
opinions	**• about yourself:** *hard-working / willing to … / good school results / energy / my dream* **• about the role:** *unexpected / unbelievable / absolutely unique experience / first step / meet professional actors*	**• about you:** *naive / no sense of reality / too self - confident / not serious / a joke / not mature enough / too young* **• about the role:** *uninteresting / manage to combine acting in a film and studies*
arguments	*acting is my dream / have always been interested in drama / lots of school plays / talented / try my luck / show what I can do*	*too young / studies first / too tiring / few successful people / unemployment / no money / hard unsteady life / no private life*
useful expressions	- *I can't wait to …* (= j'ai hâte de …) - *Please let me …* - *Great! Hurray!* - *miss an opportunity / never forgive*	*be sensible* (= être raisonnable) / *can't do two things at once* (= à la fois) / *come (back) down to earth* (= redescendre sur terre)

• Conclusion :
La décision finale des parents et la réaction qu'elle suscite doivent être indiquées soit pour clore la discussion, soit dans un commentaire ajouté.
Pense à utiliser quelques mots de liaison (***whereas, and yet, so that, as a result,…***).

More about...

... Hollywood's landmarks ► pages 64-65

1. General comprehension.

Correct these statements.

The *"Hollywood"* sign	It's a very small sign that can't be seen from a distance. ....
Grauman's Chinese theater	Very few actors have left their footprints there. .... Very few tourists are interested in seeing how actors sign their name. ....
The *Universal Studios*	Very few people visit *Universal Studios*. .... Visitors go on guided tours to watch a film being shot. ....

2. Detailed comprehension.

A The "Hollywood" sign.

What it looks like today
• its location: .... • its length: .... • its height: ....

What it looked like in the past
• It used to read "..........................." but ....were dropped in 1945. • It used to .... that had to be checked every day, but they have all been removed. • It didn't use to have .... and ....

B Grauman's Chinese Theater.

"Traces" of themselves that film stars leave in wet cement: • their .... • their .... • their ....
Name the following celebrities. • He left an imprint of his fist. .... • He left an imprint of his cigar. .... • She left an imprint of her locks. ....

C The Academy Awards Ceremony.

When?	What?	Number of people
....	The first ceremony was held.	• number of people attending the ceremony: ....
1953	....	
....	The ceremony is broadcast worldwide	• number of people attending the ceremony: .... • number of television viewers: ....

D The Academy Awards Statuette:

1. Who are the winners selected by?

....

2. What are the winners awarded?

....

3. Who was awarded a record number of Oscars?

....

4. What film won 7 miniature statuettes?

....

5. Who was nominated several times but never won?

....

6. Who is the statuette named after?

....

QUIZ

► pages 68-69

How much do you know about the United Kingdom?

1 The flag of the United Kingdom is known as:

"The Union Jack" ☐

"The Stars and Stripes" ☐

2 Great Britain is:

less populated than France ☐

more populated than France ☐

about as populated as France ☐

3 The United Kingdom is composed of:

England ☐ Scotland ☐

Wales ☐ Northern Ireland ☐

the Republic of Ireland ☐

4 Match the capitals with the different areas of Great Britain:

Edinburgh •	• Northern Ireland
Cardiff •	• Scotland
Belfast •	• Wales

5 On the picture you can see:

Tower Bridge and Buckingham Palace ☐

Tower Bridge and London's new townhall ☐

Tower Bridge and St. Paul's Cathedral ☐

6 To get to Dover from Calais you have to cross:

the North Sea ☐

the English Channel ☐

the Irish Sea ☐

7 Put these elements in chronological order (number from 1 to 3):

... the Norman Conquest

... the Roman Conquest

... the Anglo-Saxon Conquest

8 The Duke of Normandy became King of England after defeating:

the Scottish at Hadrian's Wall ☐

the Romans at Bath ☐

the Saxons at the battle of Hastings ☐

9 Since Henry VIII British monarchs:

have belonged to the Catholic Church ☐

have been Heads of the Church of England ☐

11 Britain was a republic with Oliver Cromwell at its head:

for a few years in the 16th century ☐

for a few years in the 17th century ☐

for a few months in the 17th century ☐

12 Britain became one of the wealthiest and most powerful countries in the world under the reign of:

Henry VIII ☐

Charles I ☐

Queen Victoria ☐

13 Winston Churchill was a famous:

Church leader ☐

general in WWII ☐

Prime Minister ☐

14 Put these names in chronological order (number from 1 to 10):

... Elizabeth I	... Queen Victoria
... Charles I	... Henry VIII
... Winston Churchill	... William the Conqueror
... Oliver Cromwell	... Harold
... Charles II	... Elizabeth II

Un peu de rattrapage

1. L'auxiliaire *will.* ▸ Aide : mémento, n°24

If it doesn't rain,	we**'ll go** to the beach. we**'ll be able to go** swimming. we **won't have to go** by car.
If it rains,	we **won't go** to the beach. we **won't be able to go** swimming. we**'ll have to go** somewhere else.
if + présent	valeur future

A Recopie les différentes constructions qui signifient:

- on ira … : ……………………………
- on pourra aller … :
………………………………………
- on devra aller … :
………………………………………
- on n'ira pas … : ……………………
- on ne pourra pas aller … :
………………………………………
- on n'aura pas besoin d'aller … :
………………………………………

B Complète les phrases en n'utilisant qu'une seule fois l'une des formes suivantes :

• *will* • *won't* • *will be able to* • *won't be able to* • *will have to* • *won't have to*

1. If we don't hurry, we ……………………………… be on time for the film.
2. If we arrive late, we ……………………………… see the film.
3. If I get a bad mark on my test, I ……………………………… be disappointed.
4. If you give me your CD, I ……………………………… make a copy of it.
5. If we miss the train, we ……………………………… go by car.
6. If our teacher is absent, we ……………………………… get up early tomorrow.

2. Entraîne-toi à poser des questions. ▸ Aide : mémento, n°13

Quelles sont les questions qui ont amené les réponses suivantes ?

1. …………………………………………………………………………… ?
We'll spend our next holidays [in Corsica].
2. …………………………………………………………………………… ?
I'll buy him [a camera] for his birthday.
3. …………………………………………………………………………… ?
[No,] you won't have to babysit tonight.
4. …………………………………………………………………………… ?
They'll start shooting the scene [as soon as the actors are ready].
5. …………………………………………………………………………… ?
She'll be able to give you more information [when she meets you].

Basics

① If your teacher organized an exchange ...

► pages 70-71

1. Listen and answer. ► page 70

A Ecoute les questions et coche la case de ton choix.

	Yes,please!	No, thank you.	Yes, I would.	No, I wouldn't.	I'd love to!	I'd hate it!
1.						
2.						
3.						
4.						
5.						
6.						

B Complète les phrases avec l'auxiliaire *do / does* ou *would*, selon que l'on dit ce que l'on aime faire ou ce que l'on aimerait faire.

1. .... you like to have my phone number?
2. .... you like travelling abroad?
3. Where .... you like to live when you are 20?
4. .... Brad Pitt like being photographed?
5. .... you like your teacher to organize an exchange?

2. A quiz. ► page 70

A Lis ce dialogue.

John: *If a friend asked you to borrow your computer, what would you do?*
Bob: *Since he's my friend, I'd lend him my computer.*
Kate: *Well ... I wouldn't take the risk.*
John: *Personally, I would hesitate to lend something so fragile.*

• Dans la question de John quelle est la partie de la phrase qui exprime la situation imaginaire ? ....
Le verbe conjugué .... est au ....
• Quels sont les formes verbales qui expriment la façon dont chacun réagirait face à cette situation imaginaire ?
....
L'auxiliaire utilisé est .... /......................

REMEMBER
Pour exprimer une **situation imaginaire**, on utilise *If* suivi d'un verbe conjugué au ....
Exemple : ....
Pour exprimer la réaction, le **résultat** face à cette situation, on utilise le conditionnel présent qui se forme avec l'auxiliaire .... suivi d'un verbe en ....
Exemple : ....

B **Entoure d'abord la bonne traduction de chaque verbe, puis réponds personnellement aux questions du quiz de ton manuel page 70 en cochant les cases dans la colonne de droite.**

KEEP + -ing • *cesser de* • *ne pas cesser de*	**NOT MIND** • *ne pas aimer* • *être égal*	**1.** a ☐ b ☐ c ☐ **2.** a ☐ b ☐ c ☐
MOAN • *ronchonner* • *faire ses excuses*	**DARE** • *oser* • *se plaindre*	**3.** a ☐ b ☐ c ☐
IGNORE • *faire ses excuses* • *ne pas s'occuper de*	**PRETEND** • *prêter* • *faire semblant de*	**4.** a ☐ b ☐ c ☐ **5.** a ☐ b ☐ c ☐
COMPLAIN • *se plaindre* • *faire ses excuses*	**APOLOGIZE** • *se plaindre* • *faire ses excuses*	**6.** a ☐ b ☐ c ☐ **7.** a ☐ b ☐ c ☐
LEND • *prêter* • *emprunter*	**BORROW from …** • *prêter à* • *emprunter à …*	**8.** a ☐ b ☐ c ☐

C **Dis comment tu réagirais dans les situations imaginaires suivantes en construisant des phrases sur le modèle :** *If …………………… , I would / I wouldn't …*

situation imaginaire	réaction à la situation imaginaire
1. A friend [read] my diary without my permission	be upset / (not) mind / (not) trust him / her (any more)
2. I [see] somebody hitting someone in the street	call for help / ignore them
3. I [have to spend] the night in a house that looked spooky	be excited / feel nervous / hate it / stay in the house / (not) dare to sleep there
4. Someone [draw] a silly cartoon of me	make me laugh / make me furious

1. ……………………………………………………………………………………
……………………………………………………………………………………
2. ……………………………………………………………………………………
……………………………………………………………………………………
3. ……………………………………………………………………………………
……………………………………………………………………………………
4. ……………………………………………………………………………………
……………………………………………………………………………………

3. Group work. ► page 70

A Réagis aux affirmations suivantes, en exprimant une différence ou une similitude.

1. – If I were the principal of my school, I would let students wear caps in class.
   – .... !
2. – If I were offered to play the role of an extra in a film, I wouldn't particularly like it.
   – .... !
3. – If I were a teacher I would be very strict.
   – .... !
4. – If I were asked to make a speech, I would refuse.
   – .... !

B Dans le texte ci-dessous, souligne les verbes au prétérit puis classe-les selon leur valeur.

I met her during the holidays and I fell in love with her. I gave her my address but she never wrote me. I'd be so happy if I received a letter from her! If she loved me, she would write to me. Would she even remember me if I phoned her?

situation réelle	situation imaginaire
....	....
....	....
....	....
....	

Tu remarques que le prétérit associé à *If* n'a pas de valeur temporelle. Il renvoie à une situation qui n'existe pas dans la réalité :

She wrote me … implique: *I got a letter from her*
(Elle m'a écrit…) *(yesterday / last week / last month …).*

If she wrote me… implique: *I haven't received any letters from her.*
(Si elle m'écrivait…)

C Complète ces débuts de phrases au prétérit avec *if* ou *when*.

1. .... I were invisible
2. .... I was little
3. .... I were born in the 19th century
4. .... I were not in this school
5. .... I arrived in this school
6. .... I spoke English fluently

4. Listen and make comments. ▶ page 70

Tu vas entendre six phrases pour lesquelles deux propositions te sont faites. Coche la case qui correspond à une réponse logique.

HAVE TO ... = necessary BE ABLE TO ... = possible	1.	2.	3.	4.	5.	6.
I would have to ...						
I wouldn't have to ...						
I would be able to...						
I wouldn't be able to ...						
	[speak]	[see]	[make]	[go shopping]	[go]	[practise]

REMEMBER

présent	prétérit	futur	conditionnel
can	....	....	....
has / have to	....	....	....

5. Reported speech. ▶ page 71

*"How old **is she**?"*
→ *I wonder how old **she is**.*

*"**Does she work** here?"*
→ *I wonder if **she works** here.*

REMEMBER

Le verbe *wonder* (se demander) se comporte comme le verbe *ask* (demander).
Au style indirect :
- l'ordre des mots de la phrase est celui d'une phrase déclarative ☐ interrogative ☐ ;
- lorsqu'il n'y a pas de mot interrogatif, la question indirecte est introduite par ......

Bruce est à une soirée et a remarqué une fille qu'il n'avait jamais vue auparavant. Lis les questions qu'il s'est posées, puis commente-les par des phrases commençant par : *He wondered* ... Respecte la concordance des temps.

Who's this girl? Does she like dancing? Where does she live? Has she got a boyfriend?

1. ....
2. ....
3. ....
4. ....

Oral practice

► page 71

A Ecoute et repère les syllabes accentuées dans les mots suivants :

ABROAD ALONE ABOVE AGAIN AGREE APOLOGIZE

BEFORE BETWEEN BEHIND BECAUSE

Dans tous ces mots la première syllabe est accentuée ☐ n'est pas accentuée ☐ .

B D'autres mots commençant par la première syllabe *a-* ou *be-* sont également accentués sur la deuxième syllabe. Cherche dans le lexique du manuel pages 162 et 163 :

- 11 autres verbes commençant par la syllabe *a-* non accentuée :

apologize ....

....

....

- 4 adjectifs commençant par la syllabe *a-* non accentuée :

....

....

(*accurate* est accentué sur la première syllabe)

- 4 verbes commençant par la syllabe *be-* non accentuée :

....

....

Listening

► page 71

1. Listening comprehension.

A

1. Diana notices a boy because he is attractive. Yes ☐ No ☐

2. It's the first time Marion has seen him. Yes ☐ No ☐

3. She thinks he looks ....

B

4. Diana .... if the boy lives in the neighbourhood.

5. She would be pleased ☐ She wouldn't be pleased ☐

because they .... again.

C

a. ☐

b. ☐

c. ☐

6. Marion's first suggestion: **a** ☐ **b** ☐ **c** ☐

Marion's second suggestion: **a** ☐ **b** ☐ **c** ☐

7. Diana wants to ....

8. Marion thinks it would be a good idea. Yes ☐ No ☐

because there's .... ,

so, the boy would think Diana ....

D

9. Marion thinks the boy has a girlfriend. Yes ☐ No ☐

10. Marion is interested in the boy at the door because ....

11. It's the first time the two boys have met. Yes ☐ No ☐

12. Marion ☐ Diana ☐ Marion and Diana ☐ would like to talk to the boys.

E

What questions did Diana ask herself ?

1.“..?”

2.“..?”

F

Report what Diana wonders.

3. She wonders ....

4. She wonders ....

2. Summary.

....

....

....

....

....

....

....

....

Basics

2 What would you rather do? ▶ pages 72-73

1. Pair work. ▶ page 72

A Observe ces phrases et souligne les expressions verbales avec *I'd rather*.

(1) *If I could choose, I'd rather be a director than an actor.*
(2) *I want to get as much exercise as I can. I'd rather walk than take the car.*

REMEMBER
I'd rather exprime une préférence ☐ un conseil ☐ ;
est toujours suivi d'un verbe en base verbale ☐ en *-ing* ☐ ;
est parfois suivi de *than* ☐ *that* ☐ après le verbe.

B Utilise l'expression *I'd rather...* pour compléter ces phrases de façon logique.

1. I feel a bit tired today, ... than go to the cinema.
2. .... than spend my holidays with my parents.
3. But, Mum! You know I hate spinach! .... without having dinner than eat any of this!
4. I'm afraid of animals and I hate mosquitoes. .... in a youth hostel than sleep in a tent.
5. My mum is expecting a baby. Since I already have a little brother, I .... a little sister.

2. Listen and speak. ▶ page 73

Tu vas entendre cinq situations pour lesquelles on te demande d'indiquer ta préférence en cochant la case a ou b selon le cas.

	1	2	3	4	5
a					
b					
	[live]	[spend]	[live]	[play]	[interview]

Oral practice ▶ page 73

A Ecoute l'enregistrement et souligne d'un trait toutes les syllabes qui portent un accent secondaire et de deux traits celles qui portent un accent principal.

INTRODUCE CONVERSATION INDEPENDENT UNEMPLOYMENT

INTERNATIONAL ACCOMODATION

B Maintenant, trouve par toi-même l'accent principal et l'accent secondaire des mots suivants :

DEMONSTRATION EDUCATION RESERVATION TRANSPORTATION

ACROBATIC ASTRONOMIC

Listening

1. Listening comprehension. ► page 73

A

1. Both Mike and Helena want to go out tonight ☐ tomorrow night ☐ .
2. Helena is working today. Yes ☐ No ☐
3. She is usually free at 5.30. Yes ☐ No ☐

B

4. Helena answers that she ....
....
5. Mike agrees ☐ doesn't agree ☐ .
6. They are planning to meet..
at ....

C

7. Mike is complaining because last week Helena ....
....
8. He asks her to..
9. He .... complain if she .... late.
10. Helena admits that Mike is right ☐ that Mike is wrong ☐.

D

11. Helena doesn't want to eat at ....
12. Mike doesn't want to eat at ....
13. Helena gets angry and says that Mark ....
....
14. Mark gets angry and says Helena ....

E Dictation.

1. ....
2. ....
3. ....

2. Summary.

....
....
....
....
....
....
....
....
....

Basics

3 Whoever studies English should visit Britain. ► page 74

1. Listen and speak.

A Lis les phrases suivantes :

1. (a) *I wonder **who** bumped into my car.* (b) ***Whoever** it is should pay for the damage.*
2. (a) *This is **where** we had delicious pizza.* (b) ***Wherever** we went, we had great food.*
3. (a) *I don't agree with **what** he says.* (b) ***Whatever** he says is nonsense.*
4. (a) *Be careful **when** you touch this lamp.* (b) ***Whenever** you touch it, it falls.*

Si l'on ajoute .... à, *who, where, what* ou *when* leur sens est modifié :
dans les phrases **(a)**, il s'agit d'un fait précis ☐ d'un fait plus général ☐;
dans les phrases **(b)**, il s'agit d'un fait précis ☐ d'un fait plus général ☐.

REMEMBER
.... = chaque fois que
.... = qui que ce soit, toute personne qui
.... = quelque soit l'endroit
.... = quoique ce soit

B Tu vas entendre six phrases ; coche le composé en *WH-ever* qui permet de reformuler les mêmes phrases.

	1.	2.	3.	4.	5.	6.
whoever						
wherever						
whenever						
whatever						
	[go]	[drive]	[play]	[do]	[visit]	[go hiking]

C Construis des phrases en remettant dans l'ordre les éléments donnés.

1. my bike / is / broken / Whenever / Sarah / something / brings back
....
2. they / something / about / go / Wherever / they / complain / always
....
3. at school / is threatened / Whoever / the head teacher / should tell / by somebody
....
4. my teachers / my mum / Whatever / agrees / I say about / never
....

2. What about you?

Ecoute les phrases et choisis la proposition qui correspond le mieux à tes propres réactions.

1. Whenever I get a good mark, ... a. ☐ b. ☐ c. ☐
2. Whenever I feel depressed, ... a. ☐ b. ☐ c. ☐
3. Whenever I get home late, ... a. ☐ b. ☐ c. ☐
4. Whenever I have a test, ... a. ☐ b. ☐ c. ☐

 ▶ page 75

1. Hidden words.

A **Find nine words from the list.**

B	U	V	S	T	I	G	H	T	A	E
I	N	O	I	T	C	E	R	B	L	U
D	I	U	Z	O	O	N	C	B	T	R
S	I	L	E	B	T	U	A	N	R	B
W	O	U	R	S	T	N	S	A	E	V
V	E	P	R	I	O	D	U	T	N	T
D	R	P	F	I	N	L	A	E	D	E
G	I	R	H	T	A	O	L	E	Y	D
H	E	S	I	L	K	O	T	R	U	N
K	A	R	T	I	O	S	B	U	L	D
F	A	L	P	W	L	E	X	H	U	E

....

....

....

....

....

....

....

....

....

B **Complete the sentences with some of the words you have just learnt.**

1. Clothes made of .... keep you warm; T-shirts made of .... keep you cool; clothes made of .... feel soft; shoes made of soft .... are comfortable.

2. At weekends most people like to relax and wear .... clothes, except for special occasions, like weddings, when guests are sometimes expected to come in ....

3. If a pair of jeans is too small, they don't .... because they're not the right .... and they're probably too ....

4. I look awful in this dress. It's my size but it doesn't .... me at all.

5. My parents and I never agree about clothes. When they say something is .... , I say it's not classy at all! When they say something is fashionable, I say it's been .... for at least ten years.

3. Coin New Words.

A Give definitions.

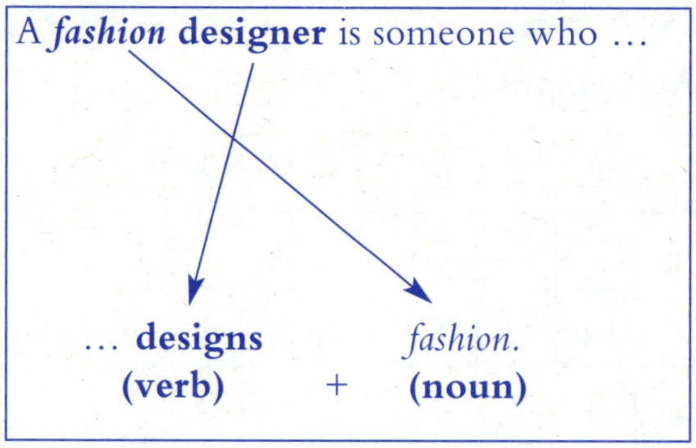

1. A music lover is ....

2. A bookseller is ....

3. A churchgoer is ....

4. A can opener is ....

5. A hair-dryer is ....

B What's the English for:

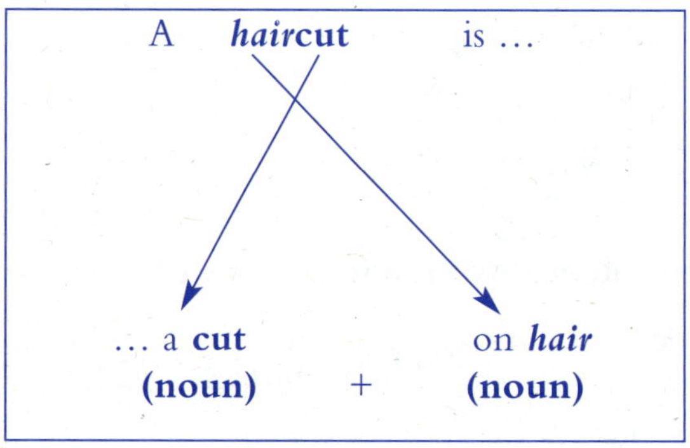

1. une empreinte de la main : ....

2. un correspondant dans un échange : ....

3. la tolérance zéro : ....

4. la langue maternelle : ....

5. une auberge de jeunesse ....

Topic

The British and fashion ► pages 76-77

1. Comprehension. ► page 76

A Are these sentences True (T) or False (F)? Justify your answers by quoting from the text.

Introduction.

1. Unusual ways of dressing are often seen in the streets of London. T ☐ F ☐

....

2. English fashion designers are influenced by the way ordinary people dress. T ☐ F ☐

....

Helen

3. At weekends, she sometimes wears her school uniform. T ☐ F ☐

....

4. She dresses differently with different people. T ☐ F ☐

....

5. She can express different aspects of her personality through her clothes. T ☐ F ☐

....

6. Her parents' tastes in clothes are the same as hers. T ☐ F ☐

....

7. Her parents criticize her all the time about what she's wearing. T ☐ F ☐

....

8. She spends a fortune on clothes. T ☐ F ☐

....

9. She only buy new clothes. T ☐ F ☐

....

10. Brand names clothes make everyone look different. T ☐ F ☐

....

B Paul : Complete these sentences:

11. Britain is different from other countries because:
people never ....and young people feel ....
....

12. Wearing eccentric clothes is a way of .... ,
of ....

13. When Paul was younger, his parents ....

14. On the picture of Paul today, his hair is .... ; so we can imagine it was .... when he was 15.

2. Find the English for :

• une façon de s'habiller :	• d'occasion :................................
• pas étonnant que ... :	• marque de vêtement :.....................
• styliste / couturier :	• arriver à / se débrouiller pour : ....
• avoir envie de :	• se faire remarquer : ....
• ça dépend de ....:	• en vieillissant : ....
• faire des essais :	• ça passe (ça s'arrête) : ....
• forme :	• coupe de cheveux : ....
• un tas d'argent :	• faire des histoires à propos de : ....
• avoir l'occasion de :	
• marché aux puces :........................	

3. Linking word. ► page 77

I can experiment with colours, shapes and designs
***as long as** I don't have to spend loads of money.*

A Match each linking word with its translation.

and yet • • *du moment que*
so that • • *et pourtant*
as long as • • *pour que*

B Connect the phrases in A and B with one linking word and complete the grid .

A		B
1. Helen is very interested in fashion	**as long as**	**1.** they can get new ideas for their collections.
2. Helen doesn't mind wearing a school uniform ...		**2.** she doesn't spend a lot of money on clothes.
3. Dress designers watch people in the street	**and yet**	**3.** she can dress as she likes at weekends.
4. Some young people say they want to be different		**4.** they wear brand name clothes that make them all look the same.
5. Helen's parents never like what she's wearing	**so that**	**5.** people will turn their heads and notice them.
6. Sometimes teenagers wear very unusual clothes		**6.** they don't usually make comments.

A1 .... B...	A2 .... B...	A3 .... B...
A4 .... B...	A5 .... B...	A6 .... B...

4. Reading aloud. ► page 77

■ **Get ready to read this part of the text aloud.**

Looking different is also young people's way of rebelling. It's their way of saying, "I don't want to be like you". But as you get older, you get over it. I remember the fuss my own parents made over my haircut when I was 15, and look at me now ...

5. Writing task. ► page 77

Imagine an argument between a teenager and his / her parents about the way s/he is dressed.

Quelques conseils.

Reporte-toi aussi à la page 71 pour suivre les conseils donnés pour rédiger l'introduction et la présentation. Voici quelques suggestions pour étoffer le contenu.

La scène est plus vivante si tu fais intervenir un père et une mère.

FATHER	MOTHER	TEENAGER (YOU)
• *silent at the beginning* • *just stares at you*	usual comments: • should get up earlier / not the only one in the family using the bathroom / shouldn't spend so much time getting ready • don't have to wear so much make up / hair isn't brushed ...	• in a good / bad mood • didn't get enough sleep • excited / worried about... • in a hurry / friends waiting for you
• *suddenly notices your clothes and your new hair style: surprised, amazed, shocked* • *very strict : change clothes at once / not appropriate for school*	• surprised at your father's reaction / doesn't agree • says it is trendy / fashionable / it's what teenagers wear nowadays / it suits you	• angry / a little offended (*vexé*) • pretend to be indifferent • accept / refuse to change clothes / ask why
opinion: • *doesn't suit you : colour and design / too tight / loose / casual / a bit eccentric* • *want to attract people's attention* • *horrified at the idea of second-hand clothes : dirty / may be full of germs* (microbes)	opinion: • agrees with you • doesn't like brand names (look the same / like a billboard) / wouldn't like you to spend much money on clothes • second-hand clothes: original way of dressing / artistic	opinion: • don't have the same tastes • interested in second-hand clothes and flea market / not interested in fashion magazines • want to feel free to express yourself through clothes / want to "be me".

More about...

UNIT 5

... places worth visiting along the river Thames. ► pages 78-79

1. General comprehension.

A Eton and Oxford:

	Eton	Oxford
Date of foundation	....	....
Reputation	One of the .... in the world.	One of the .... in the world.
How students are selected	....	....
Age of students	....	university students
Facts and Figures	• number of students: .... • academic results: .... • discipline: .... • cost per student a year: .... • number of Prime Ministers that studied there:	• three examples of the varied subjects studied: – .... – .... – .... • study conditions: .... • sporting event with Cambridge: .... • the term "Oxbridge" refers to ....

B Windsor Castle:

1. How many residences does the Royal Family own? ....

2. How many people does the Royal Family employ? ....

3. How does the Royal Family pay for its expenses?

....

4. What part of Windsor Castle would you visit if you were interested in art?

....

5. What would you visit if you wanted to see where many Royals are buried?

....

C Greenwich: complete the table with the missing information.

	In the City of Greenwich	In the port of Greenwich
What can be seen?	On the ground, in the garden of the Royal Observatory, the .... , materialized by	A famous clipper, the ....

D The Globe Theatre.
Correct these statements.

1. Very few people went to the theatre in Shakespeare's time.

....

2. Only the wealthiest people could afford it.

....

Tick the correct answers.

In the theatre today ...	whereas in Shakespeare's time ...
1. there are female and male actors,	☐ there were only female actors. ☐ there were only male actors.
2. the lighting is often elaborate,	☐ there was no lighting at all. ☐ they used candles.
3. there are afternoon and night performances,	☐ there were only day performances. ☐ there were only night performances.
4. there are performances all year round,	☐ they only took place in the summer. ☐ there were only performances in the spring.
5. the people in the audience doesn't throw things at actors,	☐ they did when they didn't like the play. ☐ they did when the play was too long.
6. it doesn't rain inside,	☐ in the Globe Theatre it did because the roof had a hole (*un trou*) in it. ☐ in the Globe Theatre it did because there was no roof.

QUIZ

► pages 82-83

How much do you know about Australia?

1 The capital of Australia is:

- Sydney ☐
- Melbourne ☐
- Canberra ☐

2 Compared to Canada, Australia is:

- less populated ☐
- more populated ☐
- as populated ☐

3 Australia's nickname is "Down Under" because Australia is:

- in the Northern hemisphere ☐
- in the Southern hemisphere ☐

4 In Australia December is:

- colder than July ☐
- hotter than July ☐

5 The Outback is:

- very populated ☐
- not very populated ☐
- a green area ☐
- a dry area ☐

6 The Great Barrier Reef is famous for:

- its rocks ☐
- its coral ☐

7 The railway line from Sydney to Perth runs along:

- about 4,500 km ☐
- about 6,000 km ☐

8 Which of the two Territories is the smallest:

- Northern Territory ☐
- Australian Capital Territory ☐

9 The Dutch and the Portuguese discovered:

- the eastern coast ☐
- the western coast ☐

The English discovered:

- the eastern coast ☐
- the western coast ☐

10 The first British settlers were:

- farmers ☐
- sailors ☐
- prisoners and soldiers ☐

11 Many new settlers arrived:

- in the 17th century Yes ☐ No ☐
- in the 1850s Yes ☐ No ☐
- in the mid 20th century Yes ☐ No ☐

12 After the WWII, most immigrants were:

- British Yes ☐ No ☐
- Asian Yes ☐ No ☐
- European but not British Yes ☐ No ☐

13 The "Aussies" is the nickname given to:

- the Australian animals ☐
- the Australian citizens ☐

15 The Aborigines have lived in Australia for:

- about fifty centuries ☐
- about five hundred centuries ☐

16 They have been Australian citizens for:

- about fifty years ☐
- about five centuries ☐

Un peu de rattrapage

1. Comparatif et superlatif. ► Aide : mémento, n°10

A Complète le tableau suivant.

adjectif ou adverbe de base	comparatif de supériorité *(plus … que)*	superlatif *(le plus …)*
popular	....	....
cheap	....	....
big	....	....
far	....	....
bad	....	....
good / well	....	....

Comparatif d'égalité et d'inégalité.

aussi … que : → **as** + *adjectif* + **as**
moins que : → **not as** + *adjectif* + **as** / **less** + *adjectif*

B Complète les phrases à l'aide des adjectifs suivants au comparatif :

• *far* • *hot* • *cold* • *dry* (sec) • *populated* (peuplé)

1. Which city is .... away from the Tropic of Capricorn: Melbourne or Sydney?
2. In the Northern hemisphere July is .... December, whereas in the Southern hemisphere July is .... December.
3. The towns in the desert are .... the cities along the coast because the climate is .... and the land is arid.

2. Entraîne-toi à poser des questions. ► Aide : mémento, n°13

Pose les questions dont les réponses sont les expressions entre crochets.

1. Gold was discovered in Australia [in the 1850s].
   ....
2. The Portuguese discovered [the western coast of Australia].
   ....
3. [Captain James Cook] discovered the eastern coast of Australia.
   ....
4. The flight from Paris to Sydney lasts [for more than 20 hours].
   ....
5. You will have a stopover (*escale*) [in Hong Kong].
   ....
6. If I could afford it, I would visit [Kakadu National Park].
   ....

UNIT 6

Basics

1 More and more changes are taking place in Australia. ▸ pages 84-85

1. Listen and compare. ▸ page 84

A **Coche la case qui te semble logique, comme dans le premier exemple.**

	1.	2.	3.	4.	5.	6.	7.	8.
+ more	✔							
- fewer								
- less								

B **Observe les exemples suivants puis complète le tableau *Remember*.**

more Australian wine
more space
more kangaroos
more students

fewer beaches
fewer koalas

less imported wine
less space

REMEMBER *more* est suivi d'un nom :	*fewer* est suivi d'un nom :	*less* est suivi d'un nom :
singulier dénombrable ☐	singulier dénombrable ☐	singulier dénombrable ☐
pluriel dénombrable ☐	pluriel dénombrable ☐	pluriel dénombrable ☐
singulier indénombrable ☐	singulier indénombrable ☐	singulier indénombrable ☐
Exemples : • .... •	Exemple :	Exemple : ....

C **Complète par *fewer* ou *less*.**

.... farmers
.... time
.... forests
.... work

.... immigrants
.... rain
.... attention
.... jobs

2. Make comments. ▶ page 84

A Indique comment les choses évoluent en utilisant le verbe *increase* ou *decrease*.

1. The world population ....
2. The number of farmers in Europe ....
3. Life expectancy (*espérance de vie*) ....

B *Million, hundred, thousand ...* ▶ Aide : mémento, n°1

• **Que peux-tu dire sur les mots soulignés ?**

19 million inhabitants *3 hundred miles* *50 thousand years* Ils sont tous précédés .... Ils ne prennent pas la marque du .... Ils se comportent comme des noms ☐ des adjectifs ☐	*millions of sheep* *hundreds of birds* *thousands of insects* Ils sont ☐ ne sont pas ☐ précédés d'un nombre. Ils sont au singulier ☐ au pluriel ☐. Ils sont suivis de la préposition .... Comment traduis-tu ces expressions ? ....

• **Dis en anglais :**

1. Il y a 20 millions de kangourous en Australie.
   ....
2. Des millions d'immigrants sont arrivés après la Seconde Guerre Mondiale.
   ....
3. Il y a plus de trois cents langues Aborigènes.
   ....
4. Des milliers de touristes visitent Ayers Rock chaque année.
   ....

3. Draw conclusions. ▶ page 84

Complète les phrases suivantes par le double comparatif approprié.

1. English is now the international language, that's why .... people speak English.
2. The influence of France is not as strong as it used to be, that's why .... people learn French.
3. People need their cars to get to work, that's why .... oil (*pétrole*) has to be imported.
4. People have .... time to cook, that's why they buy .... frozen food.

4. Make comments. ► page 85

■ Observe les exemples suivants puis complète le tableau *Remember* :

more and more polluted	*easier and easier*	*less and less interesting*
better and better	*worse and worse*	*bigger and bigger*
more and more nervous	*less and less difficult*	*farther and farther*

REMEMBER
Formation du double comparatif.
« de plus en plus … » : ………………………………………… (adjectif long)
« de plus en plus … » : ………………………………………… (adjectif court)
« de plus en plus … » : ………………………………………… (*good*)
………………………………………… (*bad*)
………………………………………… (*far*)
« de moins en moins … » : ………………………………

5. Listen. ► page 85

■ Écoute cinq questions et écris la réponse qui te semble logique.

1. …………………………………………………………………
2. …………………………………………………………………
3. …………………………………………………………………
4. …………………………………………………………………
5. …………………………………………………………………

6. Reported speech. ► page 85

A Complète les phrases au style indirect en respectant la concordance des temps :

"I have to take the train."
He says that he …………. to take the train.
He said that he…………. to take the train.

"What time does the train leave?"
He asks what time the train …………………
He asked what time the train ………………

"I can take the next train."
He says that he …………. take the next train.
He said that he …………. take the next train.

"Will I arrive on time?"
He wonders if he ………………… arrive on time.
He wondered if he ………………… arrive on time.

REMEMBER
Quand le verbe introducteur est au passé, le temps du verbe des paroles rapportées est décalé vers le passé :
*He **says** the train **is** late.* → *He **said** the train ……………… late.*
*He **says** the train **will be** late.* → *He **said** the train ……………… late.*

B Complète les phrases en faisant bien attention au temps du verbe introducteur.

1. "Will the effects of global warming increase or decrease?"
   Someone asked ....
2. "Will koalas become extinct in the next fifty years?"
   Someone else asked ....
3. "Will coastal cities get more and more populated?"
   I wonder ....
4. "Australian wine is as good as French wine."
   The wine-grower said that ....
5. "What's a kangaroo farm like?"
   She wondered ....

Oral practice

► page 85

Souligne les syllabes accentuées des mots suivants :

KANGAROO MONSOON ENGINEER REFUGEE
JAPANESE CHINESE VIETNAMESE PORTUGUESE

REMEMBER
Les mots terminées par une **voyelle double** ou par la **terminaison en *-ese*** sont tous accentués sur la .... syllabe
Exceptions : *COFFEE* • *IGLOO* sont accentués sur la première syllabe.

D'après les règles d'accentuation des mots que tu as vues au cours des unités, tu peux trouver la syllabe accentuée des mots ci-dessous. Souligne-les.

ASIAN AUSTRALIAN VOLONTEER ATTACK PANIC INDIAN PACIFIC
NOMADIC EDUCATION SCIENTIFIC TRADITION TYPHOON CHIMPANZEE

Listening

► page 85

1. Listening comprehension.

A

1. Daniel's room is getting .... and ....
2. He says it's normal because he has ....
   and ....
3. There are piles of things all over the floor. Yes ☐ No ☐

B

4. Daniel's mother would like him to .... in his cupboard.
5. He says his cupboard is too small ☐ / too messy ☐ because he got it five years ago ☐. / at the age of five ☐.
6. His father promised to buy ☐ to make ☐ a new cupboard.
   He kept his promise. Yes ☐ No ☐

C

7. Daniel puts lots of things ....
Daniel ☐ His mother ☐ thinks it's a problem because ....
.................and everything ....

D

8. Daniel says he ....
9. He has already ☐ never ☐ said it before.
10. He did it. ☐ He didn't do it. ☐
Why? Because ....
11. When will he do it?
....

E **Report what they said.**

1. Daniel said ....
2. His mother asked him ....
3. He promised ....

What were their own words?

4. Daniel's father: " ...."
5. Daniel: " ...."

2. Summary.

....
....
....
....
....
....
....

② What have they been doing? ► pages 86-87

1. Make comments. ► page 86

A Complète le tableau en mettant l'auxiliaire *be* au *present perfect*.

1. They **are** scuba diving.	**1.** They **have been** scuba div**ing**.
2. What's going on?	**2.** ....
3. I'm having a shower.	**3.** ....
4. We're revising for our exam.	**4.** ....
5. Why are you working so late?	**5.** ....

B Observe les légendes des dessins.

a. *She is painting.*

b. *She has been painting.*
c. *Her hair is full of paint.*

a. *He is running.*

b. *He has been running.*
c. *He is out of breath.*

Les phrases **a** expriment une activité en cours ☐.
une activité qui vient de se terminer ☐.

Les phrases **b** expriment une activité en cours ☐.
une activité qui vient de se terminer ☐.

Les phrases **c** expriment une trace, un indice de l'activité qui a eu lieu.

REMEMBER
Le *present perfect* en *be* + *–ing* exprime :
- qu'une activité ....
- qu'on le sait parce que ....
Exemple : ....

C Complète les phrases par un verbe au *present perfect* en *be* + *–ing*.

1. The ground is wet: it ....
2. You've got chocolate on your face: you ....
3. My bottle of perfume is empty! Who .... ?
4. I've left ten messages on your mobile: I.................................... you all day!

2. Listen. ► page 87

■ Écoute cinq situations et coche la phrase qui te semble logique.

1. My little brother is tired. a. ☐ b. ☐
2. Our neighbours are upset again! a. ☐ b. ☐
3. Our English teacher is very pleased with us. a. ☐ b. ☐
4. We're wet. a. ☐ b. ☐
5. I am furious. a. ☐ b. ☐

3. Classwork. ► page 87

■ Les phrases ci-dessous ne sont pas logiques. Corrige soit la première soit la seconde partie de chacune d'elles.

1. John *has bags under his eyes* because *he's been cooking.*

....

2. Mary *has lost her voice* because *she has been sunbathing.*

....

3. I am *out of breath* because *I've been studying.*

....

Oral practice

► page 87

■ Écris la forme "d'insistance" des verbes dans les phrases suivantes puis entraîne-toi à lire les deux formes.

1. I am exhausted. .... !
2. I'll do it .... !
3. I like it . ... !
4. She's finished. .... !
5. He wrote me a letter. .... !

Listening

► page 87

1. Listening comprehension.

A

1. Who is calling? Tracey ☐ Steve ☐
2. Where are they and what time is it?

	London	Sydney	1.00 p.m.	3.00 a.m.
Steve				
Tracey				

B

3. Steve wonders what ....

4. Tracey is surprised and angry ☐ surprised and pleased ☐.

5. Who has been working? Steve ☐ Tracey ☐

Why? ....

C

6. From Tracey's tone of voice, Steve realizes that there is a problem.

He says," .... "

" .... "

7. Tracey has been thinking about ....

D

8. What three problems does she mention?

(a)... too much.

(b). .... together.

(c). .... with each other lately.

9. What decision has Tracey taken? She ....

E

10. Steve is puzzled and disappointed ☐ puzzled and suspicious ☐.

11. He agrees with her about one of the problems she mentioned. Which one?

(a) ☐ (b) ☐ (c) ☐

12. He refuses to talk about the problem. ☐

He wants to talk about the problem now. ☐

He wants to talk about the problem later. ☐

13. She refuses. ☐ She accepts. ☐

14. For Steve, it's the middle of the day and yet he says, " .... "

For Tracey, it's the middle of the night and yet she says, " .... "

F **Dictation.**

1. ....

2. ....

3. ....

2. Summary.

....

....

....

....

....

....

....

....

Basics

3 He's been driving for 7 hours. ► page 88

1. Listen. ► page 88

A Complète avec les expressions que tu entends.

1. I've been in this school ....
2. My parents have been in France ....
3. I haven't seen Vanessa ....
4. I have known David ....
5. Kate has wanted to be a doctor ....
6. I have had these shoes ....

REMEMBER
• *for* introduit une expression indiquant une durée ☐ un point de départ ☐.
Exemple : ....
• *since* introduit une expression indiquant une durée ☐ un point de départ ☐.
Exemple : ....

B Complète par *for* or *since*.

1. .... I was born
2. .... five years
3. .... WWII
4. .... the arrival of settlers
5. .... 50,000 years
6. .... last Monday
7. .... 5.00 p.m.
8. .... I was little

C Complète les expressions en utilisant une durée. ► Aide : mémento, n°2

from 10.45 to 11.15 = for ....
from 9.30 to 11.00 = for ....
from 11.00 to 12.00 = for ....
from 1.00 to 5.00 = for ....

2. What about you? ► page 88

D'après les réponses, quelles sont les questions logiques qui ont du être posées?

1. — ....?[learn]
   — Since I was 11.
2. — .... ? [play]
   — Since I was offered a tennis racket.
3. — .... ?[collect]
   — Since the French francs disappeared.
4. — .... ?[live]
   — Since my parents bought our house.

3. Pairwork. ► page 88

A Regarde les dessins et coche les réponses.

*How long **has** it **been** rain**ing**?*

(1) *It **is raining**.*

(2) *It **has been raining** for 6 days.*

(3) *It **has been raining** since Monday.*

Quel(s) dessin(s) illustre(nt) une activité en cours ? 1 ☐ 2 ☐ 3 ☐

Lequel ne mentionne ni la durée ni le point de départ de l'activité ? 1 ☐ 2 ☐ 3 ☐

Quel verbe est au présent de *be+ -ing* ? 1 ☐ 2 ☐ 3 ☐

Lequel mentionne la durée de l'activité ? 1 ☐ 2 ☐ 3 ☐

Lequel mentionne le point de départ de l'activité ? 1 ☐ 2 ☐ 3 ☐

Quels verbes sont au *present perfect* en *be+ -ing* ? 1 ☐ 2 ☐ 3 ☐

REMEMBER

Lorsque l'on décrit une activité en cours et qui a commencé depuis un certain temps,

• si l'on mentionne sa durée, le verbe est au .... suivi de la préposition ....

• si l'on mentionne le moment où elle a commencé, le verbe est au .... suivi de ....

• si l'on pose la question, celle-ci commence par .... et le verbe est au ....

B Commente ces dessins soit au présent en *be + -ing* soit au *present perfect* en *be+ -ing* suivi de *for*... ou de *since*... et en utilisant les éléments mentionnés.

1. [call]

Sue .... a friend.

She .... a friend .... 5.00.

She................................ a friend ....20 minutes.

2. [operate on someone]

The surgeon .... *three hours.* *He* .... *He* .... *9.30.*

3. [follow]

The detective .... *a suspect.* *He* .... *four days.* *He* .... *Monday.*

C Dis en anglais.

1. Qui attends-tu ?

....

2. Depuis combien de temps attends-tu ?

....

3. J'attends depuis presque une demi-heure, depuis exactement 2h15.

....

....

More Words

► page 89

1. Hidden words.

Can you find six words from the list hidden in this snake?

....
....

2. What are they?

1. "We are the only food koalas eat." ....
2. "I am the thickest part of a tree." ....
3. "Some say I can be found in markets." ....
4. "No one invites us to their picnics, but we love sweet food so much!"
....
5. "We can often be found where there's water around." ....
6. "We are the nasty cousins of the wind." ....

3. Coin New Words. ► page 89

A With the help of the words given in the box, find the English for:

verbs:	nouns:
• *sleep*	• *suit*
• *fish*	• *machine*
• *answer*	• *bag*
• *shop*	• *centre*
• *bathe*	• *licence*

un permis de pêche : ....
un répondeur téléphonique : ....
un centre commercial : ....
un sac de couchage : ....
un maillot de bain : ....

B Cross out the 3 expressions which are not compound words (*noms composés*):

hiking boots — a meeting place — a washing machine — Sleeping Beauty
an exciting idea — dancing training — a gambling house — a tiring trip

Topic

► pages 90-91

Growing up in the Outback

1. Comprehension. ► page 90

A Write the following sentences about Jane's life under the appropriate heading. (lines 1 to 34)

She studied at home, in the "School of the Air".
She's been in a class with other students.
She has taken part in team sports.
She had lessons with her teachers on the "radio".
She has been studying in a boarding school.
She did her homework at her own pace.
She has had to learn how to be part of a group.
She sent her homework to her teachers through the mail.

Until the age of twelve ...

....
....
....
....

Since the age of twelve ...

....
....
....
....

B Detailed comprehension: Complete the sentences.

Paragraph 2 :

One **similarity** between students in the "School of the Air" and students in regular schools is that ....

Paragraph 3 :

One **advantage** of working at home alone is that you can ....
....

These **changes** were necessary for Jane to adapt to a regular school:

- learning ....
- waiting ....
- realizing ....

Paragraph 5 :

The **advantages** of living in the Outback:
She is able to distinguish between ....
and between ....
She is able to control herself in dangerous situations:
she doesn't ....;
she doesn't ....
She has learnt how to .... and ....

Paragraph 6 :

The importance of the Internet in the Outback:
People are .... and yet they ....

2. Find the English for :

- avoir le choix : ....
- la ville la plus proche : ....
- c'est à (...) km : ....
- jusqu'à l'âge de 12 ans : ....
- un cours particulier : ....
- une fois par semaine : ....
- cinq heures par jour : ....
- corriger, mettre une note : ....
- renvoyer quelque chose : ....
- s'adapter : ....
- à mon rythme : ....
- attendre mon tour : ....
- camarade de classe : ....
- en fait : ....
- si près de la nature : ....
- je sais ... (piloter, ...) : ....

3. Linking word. ► page 91

Even though we're isolated, we're in contact with people from everywhere.

A Match each linking word with its translation.

even though •	• *le résultat, c'est que …*
so that •	• *même si …*
as a result •	• *pour que …*

B Connect the phrases in A and B with one linking word and complete the grid.

A		B
1. She doesn't panic when she sees a bushfire		**1.** she could talk directly to a teacher.
2. She had one-to-one lessons on the radio	**even though**	**2.** it was difficult for her to adapt to a regular school.
3. She sent her homework to the teachers	**so that**	**3.** they could mark it.
4. She used to study alone		**4.** she is only 15.
5. She enjoyed living in the Outback	**as a result**	**5.** she knows it is dangerous.
6. She knows how to co-pilot a helicopter		**6.** she was isolated

A1 .... B…	A2 .... B…	A3 .... B…
A4 .... B…	A5 .... B…	A6 .... B…

4. Reading aloud. ► page 91

Get ready to read this part of the text aloud.

I used to study alone and do my homework at my own pace.
So, the first time I was told that I had only one hour to do an essay, I panicked! I had to learn more and more quickly, and also to wait for my turn to answer questions in class. It was a bit difficult for me to realize that I wasn't the only one the teacher listened to!

5. Writing task. ► page 91

A young student who used to live in the Outback has just moved to Sydney. S/he writes to friends to tell them how different life is in the city.

Quelques conseils. ► Outils méthodologiques, pages 132-133

- Choisis ton identité et celle de ton / tes ami(e)s et invente-toi une adresse à Sydney.
- Rends ta lettre plus vivante en utilisant des **exclamatives,** en posant des **questions** à ton / ta correspondant(e) ou en imaginant celles qu'il / elle se pose.
- Comme ta vie a changé, pense à utiliser ***used to / didn't use to*** pour parler de ta vie passée et aussi ***not ...any more*** pour maintenant.
- Pense aux mots de liaison : ***whereas*** (contraste) ***and yet, even though*** (contradiction) ***as a result, so that ...*** (conséquence)

• Introduction :

Dis pourquoi tu n'as pas écrit plus tôt :
- *since ... / for ... I am very busy*
- *new flat : settle in*
- *new school : buy books, uniform, etc...*

• Corps de la lettre :

1. Exprime tes sentiments (qui seront peut-être mitigés : ta nouvelle vie te plaît par beaucoup de côtés, mais tu regrettes sans doute certains aspects de ta vie passée). Quelques adjectifs pour exprimer ces sentiments :

excited • thrilled • amazed • disappointed • terrified • puzzled

2. Ordonne en paragraphes les thèmes que tu vas aborder. Par exemple : *life at school, free time, the environment.*

At school (inspire-toi du *Topic*) : *schoolmates • friends • not alone • help each other • ask for help • talk to teachers • ask questions*

BUT ... classes are noisy • difficult to concentrate • only one teacher for the whole class • teaching is less individual

Free time : *lots of things to do (shopping, fashion, clothes, cinema, discos) • visit friends • parties*

The environment : *everything close at hand • so many ... / so much ... • easy life • tempted by ...*

BUT ... It's difficult to adapt to ... noise / traffic / pollution / crowded places
I miss ... nature / animals
fortunately the beach and the sea are not far • new aspects of nature : coral reef, dolphins, fish, sharks • new activities : surfing / diving

• Conclusion :

Termine la lettre en mentionnant ton sentiment général : *happier or homesick?* Tu peux aussi finir en invitant tes amis à venir te rendre visite ou en annonçant un prochain retour dans l'*Outback*.

More about...

...the Aborigines of Australia ► pages 92-93

1. General comprehension.

A Their name.

The word "Aborigine"	The word "Kooris"
- comes from a native Australian language ☐. - was coined by European settlers in the 18th century ☐.	- is the name native Australians prefer to call themselves ☐. - is the name given to white settlers in the 18th century ☐.

B Their history.

When?	Where?	How many?
In the 18th century	In fertile areas throughout the entire continent	....
After the 18th century, until 1900	In .... in the Outback	....
Today	On lands that were lost and have been returned in part	....

2. Detailed comprehension.

A History.

What? Who? When? Consequences in the 18th and 19th centuries
Summarize some of the important events in the history of the Aborigines. ...., who arrived in the .... century, declared that the continent of Australia was "....................................". This meant that the native Australians were not considered .... As a result, the British settlers occupied .... and even .... Aboriginals like animals, forcing into .... They also .... their sacred sites. Another reason why the Aborigine population .... is that many died from .... that didn't exist before the arrival of ....

Consequences in present-day Australia
Compare the Aborigines today with other Australians. Tick what is true for the Aborigines. **1.** They live longer than ☐ don't live as long as ☐ other Australians. **2.** Their level of education is higher ☐ lower ☐. **3.** Unemployment is higher ☐ lower ☐. **4.** Alcoholism and drug abuse are higher ☐ lower ☐. **5.** The crime rate is higher ☐ lower ☐.

The policy of the Australian government in the 20th and 21st centuries
In 1967 the Aborigines .... In .... the policy of "terra nullius" was abandoned and the Aborigines were recognized as ....

B Uluru: Who? When? What?

1. Who visits it?

....

2. When is the deep red color of the rock most spectacular?

....

3. Who does Uluru belong to?

....

4. What do the owners of the rock ask tourists not to do?

....

C Aboriginal Art: Tick the right answer.

1. Rock paintings are representations of religious ideas and beliefs ☐.
political ideas ☐.

2. "Dream Time" refers to the creation of the world ☐.
the imaginary world of children ☐.

3. Aborigines believe that everything was created by supernatural beings ☐.
only humans were created by supernatural beings ☐.

4. The "Rainbow Serpent" is associated with the seasons ☐.
thunder and lightning ☐.

5. Very few visitors are allowed to visit the caves
because the paintings are considered sacred ☐.
because of scientific tests ☐.

QUIZ

► page 97

How much do you know about Ireland?

1 Which part of Ireland is independent?

Northern Ireland (Ulster) ☐
The Republic of Ireland (Eire) ☐

2 The capital of Northern Ireland is:

Dublin ☐ Belfast ☐

The capital of the Republic of Ireland is:

Dublin ☐ Belfast ☐

3 Cross the odd man out:

Galway Donegal Waterford
Cork Londonderry

4 Match each event with a date.

The Great Famine •	• 1972
The Easter Rising •	• 1649
Independence of Southern Ireland •	• 1916
The "Troubles" •	• 1921
Cromwell's army in Ireland •	• 1846-1849

5 The Irish have been Christian:

since the 5th century ☐
since the 6th century ☐
since the 8th century ☐

6 Ireland became an English colony under:

Elizabeth I ☐
Queen Victoria ☐
Elizabeth II ☐

7 The first English settlers were:

Protestant ☐ Catholic ☐

They settled:

in the North ☐ in the South ☐

8 Under Cromwell, the Catholics

were protected ☐ were persecuted ☐

9 As a result of the Great Famine, Ireland lost:

10% of the population ☐
20% of the population ☐
40% of the population ☐

10 Many Irish emigrated:

to the United States ☐
to England ☐
to Scotland ☐

11 The idea of an independent nation became popular:

after the Great Famine ☐
after the Easter Rising ☐
(Le Soulèvement de Pâques)

12 Number these events about the Easter Rising in chronological order from 1 to 4.

... Most Irish were shocked by the repression.
... Nationalists attempted to proclaim Ireland a republic.
... The leaders became heroes.
... Nationalists were executed.

13 For more than thirty years there have been riots:

in Northern Ireland ☐
in the Republic of Ireland ☐

14 Ireland has recently become:

a land of emigrants ☐
a land of immigrants ☐

15 Many computer companies have settled:

in Northern Ireland ☐
in the Republic of Ireland ☐

Un peu de rattrapage

1. Les dates : les jours ▶ Aide : mémento, n°1

■ **Complète chaque phrase avec la date appropriée, et écris-la en anglais en toutes lettres, puis en chiffres.** (Attention : les dates ne s'écrivent pas de la même façon en Grande-Bretagne et aux Etats-Unis.)

le 14 février • le 11 septembre • le 4 juillet • le 31 octobre • le 5 novembre

1. The Americans celebrate Independence Day on ....
2. The Twin Towers of the World Trade Center were destroyed on ....
....
3. Halloween is celebrated on ....
4. Valentine's Day is on ....
5. Guy Fawkes' night is celebrated on ....

2. Les auxiliaires de modalité. ▶ Aide : mémento, n°24

A Associe chaque auxiliaire de modalité à une ou plusieurs valeurs.

must • might • can • could • should • will • would

capacité : .... permission : ....
déduction : .... obligation : ....
conseil : .... futur : .... probabilité : ....
interdiction : .... conditionnel : ....

B Complète les phrases avec un auxiliaire de modalité.

1. It *is* cold in here! A window .... be open.
2. Don't wait for me tonight. I'm not sure but I .... be late.
3. No, you .... touch this button!
4. We've got a saxophone at home but no one .... play it.
5. Tell me what's the best thing to do: .... I tell the truth or not?
6. If you were me, what .... you do?

UNIT 7

Basics

1 What had they already done? ► pages 98-99

1. Look and comment. ► page 98

A Observe ces phrases.

1. **(a) Yesterday** when John **got** home, **(b)** he **did** his homework.
2. **(a) Yesterday** when John **got** home, **(c)** he **had done** his homework.

• La partie **(a)** de la phrase parle-t-elle d'un fait présent ou passé? …………………
Yesterday sert de point de référence et le verbe est au ……………………
• Dans la phrase **1** :
- John a-t-il fait ses devoirs avant de rentrer chez lui ou après ? ……………………
- le verbe de la partie (**b**) de la phrase est au ………………………………………
• Dans la phrase **2** :
- John a-t-il fait ses devoirs avant de rentrer chez lui ou après ? ……………………
- le verbe de la partie (**c**) de la phrase est formé avec l'auxiliaire ………… suivi du ………………………… Le temps de ce verbe est le …………………………

REMEMBER
Lorsque l'on parle d'un événement passé, celui-ci peut être précédé ou suivi d'un autre événement. Les verbes sont alors respectivement au :

événement précédent	ÉVÉNEMENT PASSÉ	événement suivant
………………………	*prétérit*	………………………

B Complète les phrases suivantes en utilisant le verbe indiqué au *past perfect*.

1. When we arrived at the theatre, the play ……………………………[already start]
2. Paul didn't want to see the film because he ……………………… [already see it]
3. I didn't feel hungry because I ……………………………………………… [already have dinner]
4. She felt very excited when she flew to the United States because she ………… ……………………… [never take a plane]
5. I couldn't buy any souvenirs because I ………………………………………… [spend all my money]

C Lis les affirmations ci-dessous, coche la bonne réponse en te reportant à la page 98.

1. On July 23rd they had already been to Northern Ireland. true ☐ false ☐
2. On July 13th they hadn't seen Dublin yet. true ☐ false ☐
3. On July 20th they hadn't been to the West of Ireland yet. true ☐ false ☐
4. On July 31st they had already been hiking. true ☐ false ☐
5. When they left Ireland, they had seen a hurling match. true ☐ false ☐

2. Listen and comment. ► page 99

Ecoute six situations et coche la case qui correspond à ce qui avait déjà été fait ou n'avait pas été fait quand Kate est rentrée chez elle hier soir.

	1	2	3	4	5	6
had already [done]						
hadn't [done] yet						
	[start to cook]	[have a bath]	[be set]	[call]	[park]	[read]

3. What about you? ► page 99

Dis ce que tu avais déjà fait ou ce que tu n'avais pas encore fait soit mardi soit vendredi derniers à 11 heures du matin. Coche le début de phrase que tu choisis, puis continue la phrase en utilisant les verbes proposés.

• *have breakfast* • *have lunch* • *already have a … class* (= cours de …)
• *not have a … class yet* • *see my classmates*

Last Tuesday at 11.00 a.m. ☐ Last Friday, at 11.00 a.m. ☐

1. I ....
2. I ....
3. I ....
4. I ....
5. I ....

4. Reported speech. ► page 99

Complète les phrases suivantes au style indirect :

1. "I am going to go to Dublin."
   He said that..
2. "It's not the first time I've been to Dublin."
   He said that..
3. "I go to Ireland every year."
   He said that..
4. "This year I will not go to Northern Ireland."
   He said that..
5. "I have already been there."
   He said that..

Oral practice

► page 99

A Entoure les deux dernières syllabes des mots ci-dessous et souligne la syllabe accentuée comme dans l'exemple.

I DEN TITY

[consonne] + I T Y

MAJORITY NATIONALITY CHRISTIANITY
COMMUNITY OPPORTUNITY

Tu constates que tous les mots terminés en *–ity* sont accentués sur la syllabe qui ………………… [consonne] + *ity*

REMEMBER

Voici ce que tu as appris au cours des 7 unités de ton manuel :

• Les mots terminés par ***-ic*** ***-ion*** ***-ian*** ***-ity*** sont accentués sur la syllabe qui précède ces finales.
Exemples : ……………………… ………………………
……………………… ………………………
Quatre mots courants font exception à la règle : ……………… ………………
……………… ………………

• Pour beaucoup de mots dont la première syllabe est ***a-*** ou ***be-***, cette syllabe n'est pas accentuée.
Exemples : …………………… …………………… ……………………

• Les finales en ***–er*** / ***-or*** ne sont jamais accentuées.
Exemples : ……………………… ………………………

• Les finales en ***voyelles doubles*** ou en ***–ese*** sont toujours accentuées.
Exemples : ……………………… ………………………
Deux mots courants font exception à la règle car ils sont accentuées sur la première syllabe :
Exemples : ……………………… ………………………

B Souligne les syllabes accentuées des mots suivants :

REPUBLIC CATHOLICS SOLUTION ANOTHER OTHER COFFEE CELTIC MUSIC TRADITION(AL) TELEVISION RIVER ALONG ABROAD POLITICS BECOME ADAPTER FEWER REJECTION GAELIC TECHNICIAN ENGINEER ACCEPT ALLOWED ARABIC

1. Listening comprehension.

A

1. When Samantha phoned, John had left home ☐ had come back home ☐.
2. John left home at 6. 50 ☐ 7.00 ☐ 7.10 ☐.
3. Samantha has been worrying. Yes ☐ No ☐

B

4. John left home with his money. Yes ☐ No ☐
5. Tick the right pictures.

☐

☐

☐

☐

☐

C

6. John came to Samantha's house on foot ☐ by car ☐ by bus ☐.
7. Samantha asks John to give her ....
8. He has forgotten to bring it ☐ to make it ☐.
9. John's personality: he is very ....

D What did they ask, say or think?

10. Samantha asked ....
11. John said that ....
12. John's mother said," ...."
13. Samantha thought," ...."

2. Summary.

....

....

....

....

....

....

....

Basics

2 What might have happened if things had been different? ▶ pages 100-101

1. Make comments. ▶ page 100

A What would have happened.

ce qui s'est réellement passé : *You arrived late.*	**la conséquence réelle a été :** *You didn't see the beginning of the play.*
si les choses avaient été différentes : *If you hadn't arrived late,* le verbe est formé avec : • l'auxiliaire .... • suivi du .... du verbe.	**la conséquence certaine aurait été :** *... you would have seen the beginning of the play.* le verbe est formé avec : • l'auxiliaire .... • suivi de .... + ... du verbe.

Complète de façon logique le début ou la fin de la phrase.

1. .... in a different class, I wouldn't have met you. [be]
2. .... you were free tonight, I would have bought a ticket for you too. [try]
3. .... that Ted was ill, I would have called him. [know]
4. If my parents hadn't moved, I .... schools. [have to change]
5. If I hadn't braked (*freiné*) in time, I .... into the wall. [crash]
6. If my passport hadn't been renewed, I .... go to the United States. [be able to]

B What might have happened.

ce qui s'est passé : *You arrived late.*	**la conséquence réelle a été :** *You didn't have a good seat.*
si les choses avaient été différentes : *If you hadn't arrived late,* le verbe est formé avec : • l'auxiliaire .... • suivi du .... du verbe.	**une conséquence possible aurait été :** *... you might have had a good seat.* le verbe est formé avec : • l'auxiliaire .... • suivi de .... + ... du verbe.

Pour chacune des situations ci-dessous, imagine des conséquences certaines dans le passé :

1. If my mother had seen me with those jeans on, she ....
....
2. If I had known that the teacher was absent, I ....
....
3. If my father hadn't met my mother, I ....
....

Pour chacune des situations ci-dessous, imagine des conséquences possibles dans le passé :

4. If I had bought a lottery ticket, I ....
....
5. If our goalkeeper had been better, our team ....
....
6. If my English teacher hadn't organized a trip to England, ...
....

REMEMBER

• *If* + sujet + verbe au *past perfect* exprime une hypothèse dans le passé.

Exemple : ....

• pour exprimer une conséquence certaine, on utilise .... + ... + ...

Exemple : ....

• pour exprimer une conséquence possible, on utilise .... + ... + ...

Exemple : ....

2. What wouldn't have happened? ► page 101

Regarde à nouveau les photos et leurs légendes de la page 98 de ton manuel et fais des hypothèses sur ce qui ne se serait pas passé si ....

1. If Brian hadn't been to Northern Ireland, ...
....
2. If he hadn't visited the western part of Ireland, ...
....
3. If he hadn't had any money left at the end of his trip, ...
....

3. What about you? ► page 101

Réponds aux questions suivantes. Tu peux utiliser les mots clés qui te sont proposés.

1. How would your life have been different if you had been born in the 19th century?
• *school* • *clothes* • *hobbies* • *technology* • *travelling …*

....
....
....

2. How would your life have been different if you had been born in another country?
• *language* • *mother tongue* • *eating habits …*

....
....
....

Oral practice

► page 101

*I **have** a shower every morning.*
= verbe → accentué et en forme pleine [hæv]
*I **have** taken a shower.*
= auxiliaire → non accentué et en forme réduite [əv]

Coche la prononciation du mot have dans les phrases suivantes, puis entraîne-toi à les lire à voix haute.

1. a. I don't have any cousins. [hæv] ☐ [əv] ☐
b. I have got many cousins. [hæv] ☐ [əv] ☐

2. a. We might have dinner in this restaurant. [hæv] ☐ [əv] ☐
b. We have just had dinner. [hæv] ☐ [əv] ☐

3. a. I have cooked something nice for you. [hæv] ☐ [əv] ☐
b. I have something nice for you. [hæv] ☐ [əv] ☐

4. a. What would you have? [hæv] ☐ [əv] ☐
b. What would you have done? [hæv] ☐ [əv] ☐

5. a. I have already had chocolate ice-cream. [hæv] ☐ [əv] ☐
b. Wouldn't you rather have an apple pie? [hæv] ☐ [əv] ☐

Listening

► page 101

1. Listening comprehension.

A

1. Carol wants to know ....
2. What splashed mud all over Richard? ....
3. It happened as Richard was going to the video shop ☐.
as Richard was coming back from the video shop ☐.
4. Then Richard slipped (*glisser*) and ....
5. He says, "If I ...., this ...."

B

6. Did Richard get the DVD? Yes ☐ No ☐
Because somebody ....
7. He tried to ....
8. The problem: ....
9. The explanation: "If the television .... so loud, she .... and she......................................

C

11. Carol thinks it's his fault because ....
12. She thinks that getting the DVD was possible ☐ impossible ☐.
She says, "If you .... earlier, they .... the DVD.
13. Did he know she was going to be so upset? Yes ☐ No ☐
Did he take another DVD? Yes ☐ No ☐
He says, "If I .... so upset, I .... another DVD.

D

14. Three things he's going to do:

....

15. One things they're both going to do:

....

E **Dictation.**

1. ....
2. ....
3. ....

2. Summary.

....

....

....

....

....

....

....

....

Basics

3 I wish I had taken waterproof clothing!

► page 102

1. Make comments.

A Observe les phrases suivantes.

I'm worried about Mark but ...

(**1a**) *I* ***can't*** *call him.* (**1b**) *I* ***have lost*** *his phone number.*

(**2a**) *I wish I* ***could*** *call him!* (**2b**) *I wish I* ***hadn't lost*** *his phone number!*

Les phrases (**1**) expriment une situation qui fait problème ☐ un regret ☐.
Les phrases (**2**) expriment une situation qui fait problème ☐ un regret ☐.
La phrase (**2a**) exprime un regret concernant le présent ☐ le passé ☐.
Le verbe est au ....
La phrase (**2b**) exprime un regret concernant le présent ☐ le passé ☐.
Le verbe est au ....

Comment traduirais-tu les phrases (2a) et (2b)?

(**2a**) Si seulement je pouvais l'appeler! ☐
Je pourrais l'appeler. ☐
(**2b**) Si seulement je n'avais pas perdu son numéro ... ☐
J'avais perdu son numéro ... ☐

Tu remarques le changement de forme des verbes : puisque l'on regrette une situation, on souhaite son contraire, donc les formes affirmatives deviennent des formes négatives et vice-versa. Le français fonctionne de la même façon :

Il ***pleut*** *tous les jours.* → *Si seulement il* ***ne pleuvait pas*** *tous les jours !*
Je ***n'ai pas retrouvé*** *mes clefs.* → *Si seulement j'****avais retrouvé*** *mes clefs !*

REMEMBER
Lorsque l'on exprime un regret, on peut utiliser l'expression : ....
Celle-ci est suivie :
- d'un verbe au .... lorsque l'on regrette une situation présente.
- d'un verbe au .... lorsque l'on regrette une situation passée.

B Complète les phrases avec l'expression *I wish* suivie du verbe proposé au prétérit ou au *past perfect*.

1. I'm cold. .... a warm sweater. [take]
2. Look, we can't go out because it is raining. .... [rain]
3. I haven't got any money left. .... all my money. [spend]
4. My computer is out of order (*en panne*). .... how to repair it. [know]
5. I can speak Arabic but I can't read it. .... read Arabic. [can]

More Words

► page 103

1. A puzzle.

■ Place eight words from the list in the grid.

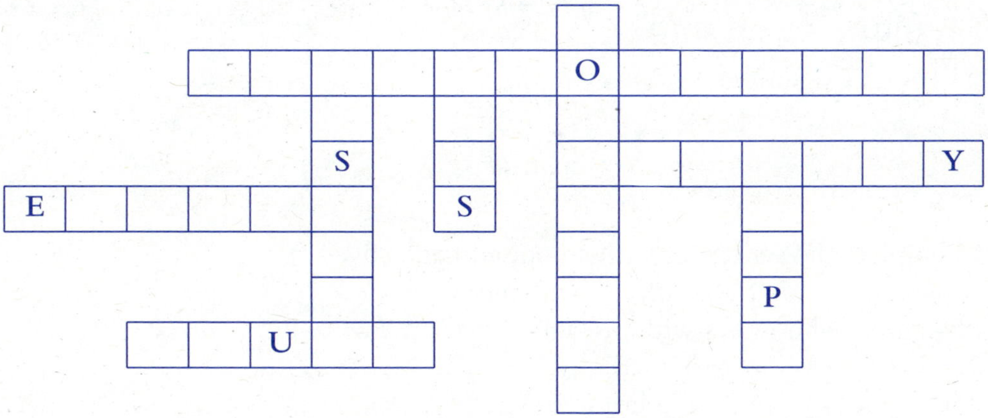

2. Some definitions.

A Complete the sentences with words from the list:

1. If an immigrant wants to work in a foreign country he must get permission. He needs a ....

2. Countries are separated by ...., where travellers are sometimes asked to show their passports. Then, they go through ...., where they are asked if they have anything to declare.

3. Many things seem strange to .... who have only recently arrived in a country or a place they have never been to before.

4. You express yourself more easily in your .... because it is your native language.

5. Many immigrants live far from their native countries. As a result, they often feel .... and they .... their families.

B What word best describes these problems that immigrants sometimes face ...

1. because of the colour of their skin? ....

2. because of constant and repeated annoyances? ....

3. because they are not accepted by other people? ....

4. because other people make unfair judgments about them? ....

UNIT 7

3. Coin New Words. ► page 103

open-minded **big-hearted** **left-handed**
red-haired **blue-eyed** **old-fashioned**

• open • big • red • blue • left • old are adjectives ☐ nouns ☐
• mind • heart • hair • eye • hand • fashion are adjectives ☐ nouns ☐

left – handed
= adj. + noun +ED

Complete the sentences with compound adjectives.

Someone who writes with his left hand is *left-handed*.

1. Someone who writes with his right hand is ....

2. Someone who has dark hair is ....

3. Someone who has "a big head" is ....

4. Someone whose mind is narrow (*étroit*) is ....

5. Someone who has nothing in his hands is empty-......................................

6. Someone who forgets many things is absent-..

Topic

An immigrant in France ► pages 104-105

1. Comprehension. ► page 104

A Introduction: Answer these questions about Conall Carr.

1. What country did he emigrate from? ....
2. What part of the country did he grow up in? ....
3. How many brothers and sisters did he have? ....
4. What does he do now? ....

B Paragraphs 1, 2 and 3: Find sentences in the text that confirm the following:

1. Conall doesn't feel like a foreigner in France.
   ....
2. He has got a strong accent in French.
   ....
3. His Gaelic is as good as his English.
   ....
4. But he doesn't speak it as well as he used to.
   ....

C Paragraphs 4: Complete these sentences:

If Conall Carr **had stayed** in Ireland, ...

1. .... foreign languages.
2. .... in the hotel business.
3. .... different jobs abroad.

D Paragraphs 5 and 6: Are these statements true (T) or false (F)? Justify your answer by quoting from the text.

1. Ireland in the late 1990s is the same as it used to be in the 1960s. T ☐ F ☐
   ....
2. Ireland is a country of emigrants. T ☐ F ☐
   ....
3. New immigrants in Ireland work as teachers, doctors or famers. T ☐ F ☐
   ....
4. Living abroad is an enriching experience if you spend a few years there. T ☐ F ☐
   ....
5. By living abroad, people get more tolerant. T ☐ F ☐
   ....

2. Find the English for :

• tenir un "pub" :	• une langue maternelle : ....
• comparé à :	• se rouiller : ....
• élever :	• l'hôtellerie : ....
• bilingue :	• un grand besoin de personnel qualifié ....
• un avantage :	• l'industrie du tourisme : ....
• un pays étranger :	

3. Linking word. ► page 91

It's not easy to find a job there, ***unless*** *you work in the tourist business.*

What's the French for *unless* : si ☐ même si ☐ sauf si ☐

A Connect the phrases in A and B with one linking word and complete the grid.

A		B
1. In the past, many Irish emigrated to other countries	**whereas**	**1.** it's not easy to find a job in the west of Ireland.
2. Some immigrants feel rejected or harassed	**unless**	**2.** you speak it at home.
3. It's easy to forget your mother tongue	**as a result**	**3.** you stay there for a few years.
4. More and more people are needed in the tourist business all over the world	**and yet**	**4.** the Irish don't have these problems.
5. There are more and more new industries in Ireland		**5.** today Ireland attracts many immigrants.
6. You can't really get to know a country		**6.** there are many job opportunities in the hotel business.

A1 .... B...	A2 .... B...	A3 .... B...
A4 .... B...	A5 .... B...	A6 .... B...

B Complete the following sentences with *if* or *unless*.

1. You won't be able to see the Cliffs of Moher .... it's foggy.
2. You won't be able to understand the lyrics of traditional Irish songs .... you speak Gaelic.
3. You can't find a place to sleep in Dublin in the summer .... you haven't booked a room in advance.
4. You can't become fluent in a foreign language .... you have spent some time in the country.

4. Writing task.

If you chose to emigrate, which country would you choose?
Explain your choice.

Quelques conseils.

• **Remarques préliminaires :**

• La façon dont la question est posée doit t'amener à te projeter dans l'avenir et à t'imaginer jeune adulte émigrant. Tu vas donc devoir imaginer les conséquences d'un tel choix sur ta vie à l'âge de 25 ans plutôt qu'à 14 ou 15 ans.

• Tu as appris beaucoup de choses sur plusieurs pays dans *New Step in 3*[e]. C'est le moment de les utiliser, et de te reporter aux chapitres précédents. Bien sûr, tu peux aussi choisir un autre pays que tu connais bien pour des raisons personnelles.

• Pense bien qu'on émigre dans un endroit particulier. Tout n'est pas vrai partout dans un pays, surtout quand il est très grand (*USA, Canada, Australia*).

• **Introduction :**
Imagine les raisons qui peuvent te pousser à vouloir quitter la France :
- *disappointed with … / bored with … / always the same … / unemployment… / politics …*
- *wish to discover new country / new culture / new people … / wish to learn a new language, to open your mind to be different …*
- *personal reasons*

• **Développement.** (les différentes suggestions ne sont pas nécessairement à mettre dans cet ordre et ne sont pas toutes obligatoires)

1. Dis dans quel pays, ou pour les plus grands, dans quelle région de ce pays tu souhaiterais vivre.

2. Dis comment tu en as entendu parler (***present perfect*** *; I have read …, heard about …, dreamt …, seen …, met people who …, already been to …*)
Tu peux dire depuis combien de temps tu envisages de partir (*I've been thinking of / planning to … for … / since …*)

3. Expose tes raisons, parmi lesquelles il peut y avoir :
- *Your likes and dislikes / your hobbies / the job you want to do :*
__As__ I am interested in … / __Since__ I've always wanted to …
- *The natural environment (climate:* utilise des **comparatifs** / *landscapes / animals*
- *New opportunities (jobs / sports)*

4. Imagine ce que cela changerait dans ta vie :
- *If I …. I would(n't) …* (certitude) / *I might …* (possibilité)
- Les contraintes que tu aurais (*I would have to …*) ou que tu n'aurais plus (*I wouln't have to … any more*)
- Les possibilités qui s'ouvriraient à toi (certaines ou non) *I would / might be able to …*

• **Conclusion:**
Tu peux terminer en disant :
– soit ce que tu as fait, les démarches que tu as entreprises (*I have already …*)
– soit ce que tu vas faire (*I'm going to …*)
– soit ouvrir la conclusion en évoquant l'avenir : *You never know … / You can't be sure … / Who knows …*

5. Let's recap.

Retrouve dans le texte du *Topic* page104 des exemples illustrant certains points de grammaire que tu as vus au cours des unités de *Step in* 3ème.

1. deux expressions avec *used to* : ....
....

2. un double comparatif : ....

3. un verbe en forme passive : ....

4. une expression avec le verbe *make* : ....

5. un gérondif après une préposition : ....

6. deux formes d'insistance : ....
....

7. un verbe au *past perfect* : ....

8. un verbe au conditionnel passé : ....

9. un souhait : ....

10. un adjectif composé : ....

More about...

... Irish culture ▶ pages 106-107

1. General comprehension.

National holiday: ...., celebrated on ....
National symbol: ....
Traditional musical instruments: ....
....
Traditional sports: ....
Main religion: .... , practised by .... % of the population.
Famous writers: ....
Languages: ....

2. Detailed comprehension.

A Complete the following grid.

Aspects of Irish culture	In the past	Today
St. Patrick's Day	**Who** converted the Irish to Christianity? .... **What** did he use to explain an important Christian idea?	**How** do the Irish celebrate St. Patrick's day? - People wear a .... or a .... - The Irish Prime Minister offers the President of the United States a ....
religious art and sculpture	**Who** produced beautiful works of religious art? **When?** .... **Where** did they live and work? .... **What** exactly did they do? .... **What** types of sculpture were produced at this time?	**What** is the name of one of the most beautifully decorated manuscripts in the world? .... **Where** is it? .... **Where** are many religious sculptures still found? ....
poetry and story telling	**Who** transmitted stories from one generation to the next? .... **What** were these stories about? .... **How** were they transmitted? in writing ☐ orally ☐	**How** does the bard tradition live on? -The Irish love to ...., to .... and .... with words. **What** famous prize have many Irish authors and poets won? The .... in ....

music	**What** two qualities were the bards admired for? - their .... - their .... **What** instrument did they play?	**What** do people enjoy doing in pubs? .... **What** kind of dances and music are still very popular? ....
sports	**What** association was created in 1884? .... **What** was its purpose?	**What** sports are popular today? Celtic sports ☐ English sports ☐ **Why** are they fun to watch? They're .... spectacles.
language	**What** language was spoken throughout Ireland? .... **When** did it begin to decline?	**What** was done to stop the decline of the language? - Many associations .... - The Republic of Ireland is .... - Road signs are .... - Irish Gaelic is ....

B Tick the right answer:

1. Where are there more Irish today?
- ☐ in Ireland
- ☐ in the US
- ☐ in England

2. Hurling can be compared to
- ☐ rugby
- ☐ hockey
- ☐ soccer

3. Gaelic football can be compared to:
- ☐ rugby
- ☐ hockey
- ☐ soccer

4. Irish monks in the Middle Ages illuminated manuscripts written in:
- ☐ Gaelic
- ☐ Latin
- ☐ English

5. On Celtic crosses there are:
- ☐ scenes from the Bible
- ☐ scenes from popular legends

6. Irish Gaelic is:
- ☐ a Germanic language like English
- ☐ a Celtic language like Welsh

It is:
- ☐ easy to read and pronounce
- ☐ difficult to read and pronounce

7. *The Canterville Ghost* is by
- ☐ Oscar Wilde
- ☐ George Bernard Shaw

Sunday, Bloody Sunday ► pages 112-113

1. Introduction.

1. What is the title of the song? ....
When was it composed? ....

2. Who wrote the lyrics? ....
Who composed the music? ....

3. The song refers to two tragic events in Northern Ireland:

a. The first took place on .... in ....
b. The people involved were ....
c. What they were doing: ....
....
d. The number of people killed: ....
e. How they were killed: . ...
f. The IRA stands for (*see page 97 in your book*): ....
g. The second event took place .... years later, in .... ,
in ....
h. The people involved were .... ;
one of them was ....
i. What they were doing and why: ....
....
j. The number of people who died: ....

4. In Northern Ireland, who supports (*see page 97 in your book*):

a. the Irish Catholics: ☐ the IRA ☐ the British troops
b. the Irish Protestants: ☐ the IRA ☐ the British troops

2. Detailed comprehension.

A Write the word from column A next to its translation in column B.

[the number in parenthesis refers to the line number of the song]

A		B
words from the song		**meaning of the word as used in the song**
march	(introduction)	.... = *grève de la faim*
trial	(introduction)	.... = *injectés de sang*
hunger strike	(introduction)	.... = *immunisés*
bodies strewn	(7)	.... = *séparés de force*
heed	(8)	.... = *tenir compte de, faire attention à*
trenches	(22)	.... = *tranchées*
dug	(22)	.... = *procès*
torn apart	(23)	.... = *larmes*
wipe	(33)	.... = *jonchés de cadavres*
tears	(33)	.... = *essuyer*
bloodshot	(34)	.... = *revendiquer*
immune	(38)	.... = *manifester*
claim	(43)	.... = *creuser*

B Answer the following questions:

1. Which question is repeated 9 times in the song?

....

The singers do this to show:

- ☐ they are tired of this war that has been going on for too long.
- ☐ no one seems to be listening to those who want the war to end.
- ☐ both of the answers above.

2. The singers emphasize that blood and violence are everywhere in different ways:

a. The word of the chorus: ....

b. The number of times it is repeated in the song: ....

c. Other words or expressions from the song:

• torn apart • bodies strewn • cry • battle call • lost • won
• trenches • die • victory • tears • bloodshot

Which words refer to war? ....
....
....
....

Which words suggest sadness? ....

Which words suggest separation? ....

C Here are different ideas expressed in the song. Find the lines and quote the text.

1. I refuse to respond to calls for violence.

   ....

2. In this war there's no winner.

   ....

3. The enemies in this war are all Irish, they all belong to the same family.

   ....

4. You're eyes are red from crying so much. It's time to stop crying.

   ....

5. The official version of facts presented on TV is false; it does not reflect reality.

   ....

6. We don't react any more. People sacrifice their lives. While we continue eating, they go on hunger strikes and die.

   ....

7. It will be very difficult to do, but we must follow in the footsteps of Jesus, refusing violence and going towards peace.

   ....

D The adjective "bloody" has three meanings:

(1) stained with blood; dripping with blood
(2) cruel, merciless
(3) in British English it is a swearword, used to emphasize an emotion such as anger or disgust.

In your opinion, which of the meanings of "bloody" is used in the expression "Bloody Sunday"?

☐ definition 1 ☐ definition 2 ☐ definition 3 ☐ all three definitions

Captain Cook ► pages 114-117

1. General comprehension.

Captain Cook's

1. date and place of birth : ....

2. date and place of death : ....

3. voyages :

	date	name of the ship/s
First voyage	....	- ....
Second voyage	....	- .... - ....
Third voyage	....	- ....

2. Detailed comprehension.

A Cook's early life.

statement	right	wrong	justification
1. Sailing was a tradition in Cook's family.			....
2. Cook went to university.			....
3. He left home and worked on a coal ship.			....
4. He joined the Royal Navy as an officer.			- .... - ....
5. His maps helped the English to conquer Quebec in 1763.			....

B The First Voyage.

Complete these sentences by quoting from the text :

1. Its aim was ....
2. On board the *Endeavor,* there were .... sailors and .... scientists and there was .... and .... for a whole year.
3. The *Endeavor's* secret mission was to ....
4. The French and the English were rivals and the English wanted to ....
5. The journey was dangerous because of the ...., but the worst problem was ....
6. The scientists were not able to observe Venus because................................ ....
7. Cook was so good at drawing map that his maps of the coastline of New Zealand ....
8. The wildlife mission was a success because the scientists ....
9. Thanks to Cook the British Empire expanded because................................ ....

Find the English for :

1. *scorbut* = ...
2. *choucroute* = ...
3. *hévéas (arbres à caoutchouc)* = ...

C The Second Expedition.

Complete the first sentence then find out what these "definitions" refer to.

1. The aim of Cook's second expedition was to find out ....
2. An instrument Captain Cook was the first navigator to use: ....
3. What Captain Cook and his crew had to fight against: ....
4. Because of it Cook wasn't able to continue his voyage to the South: ....
5. A place where Captain Cook was always welcomed: ....
6. The name of one of the many islands discovered by Cook : ....
7. The name of the people who killed the entire crew of the *Discovery*: ....
8. The feelings Captain Cook experienced when he left for England: .... and ....

D The Third and Final Voyage.

Use an atlas and your English book page 114 to write these names on the map below :

Atlantic Ocean – Cape Town – Tasmania – New Zealand – South Pacific Ocean – North Pacific Ocean – Bering Strait – North America – Asia – Baffin Bay – Greenland

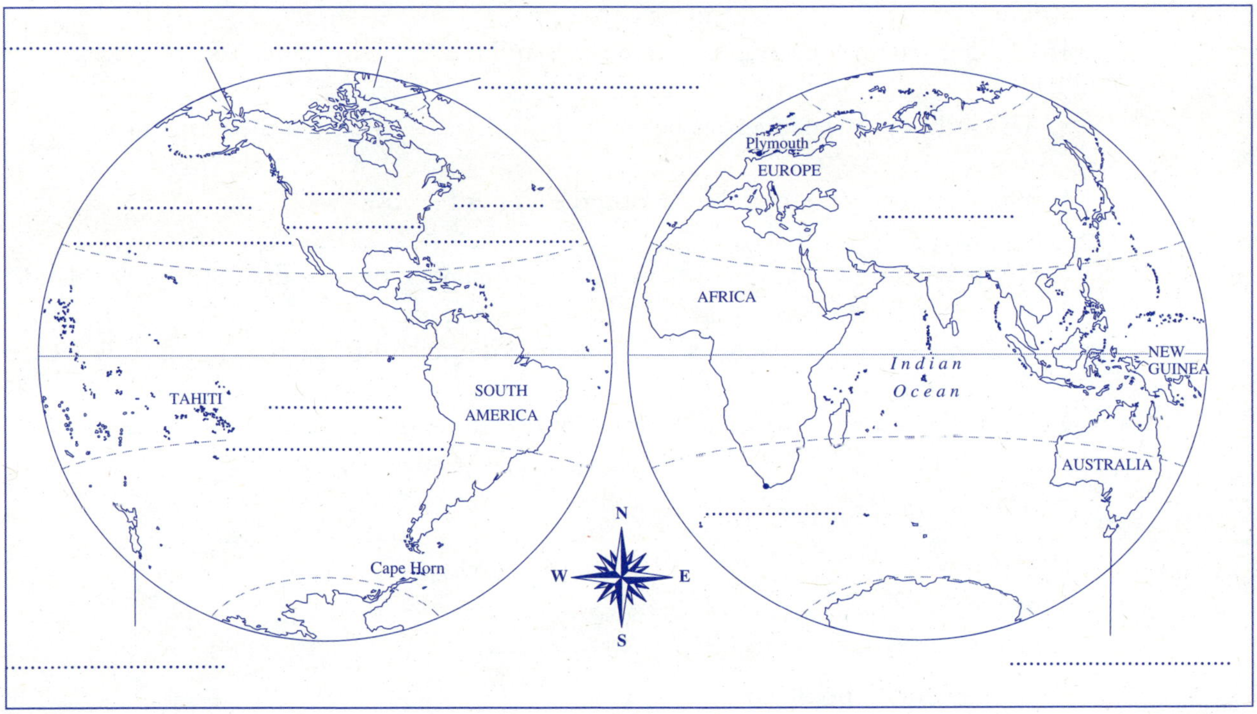

Say why the following statements are true:

1. The third expedition was to find a passage between Asia and North America.

 ....

 ....

2. The natives behaved in a friendly way in Hawaii.

 ....

 ....

3. But, in 1779, their attitude changed.

 ....

 ....

4. The Maoris felt sorry for what they had done.

 ....

 ....

5. Captain Cook's body was never sent back to England.

 ....

 ....

Frankenstein ► pages 118-123

Introduction

A Fill in the blanks.

The author, ... , married .... , and was a friend of .... , who were two famous Romantic poets.

B Answer the questions.

1. How old was she:
- **a.** when she travelled to France and Switzerland? ....
- **b.** when she began her novel? ....
- **c.** when she got married? ....
- **d.** when her book was published? ....

2. Where was she when she wrote Frankenstein? ....

3. How many people was she with? ....

Part I

A Tick the right answers.

1. Victor Frankenstein was a scientist interested in
☐ destroying people.
☐ discovering the secrets of life.

2. He realised lightning could
☐ create life from things that were dead.
☐ light up his lab.

3. He used electricity produced by
☐ clouds.
☐ flashes of lightning.

4. The lightning was caught and sent down to the machine in his lab by
☐ a mast.
☐ wires.

5. Victor Frankenstein made the body with :
☐ pieces of human bodies he had stolen.
☐ pieces of human bodies the University had given him.

B What did the monster look like?

His face ....
His skin ....
His eyes .... and ....
His lips ....
His smile ....
His legs and arms ....

Part II

Continue the story by putting these sentences in chronological order and numbering them from 1 to 8.

...... Victor Frankenstein's brother was killed.
...... Victor Frankenstein was horrified and terrified by what he saw.
...... The body was attached to the wires from the machine.
...... The monster came to life.
...... A storm came.
...... Electricity was transported through the mast to the machine.
...... Victor Frankenstein ran into town.
...... The monster escaped.

Part III

1. Where and when did Victor Frankenstein see the huge figure standing in the rain?
In the .... , during .... ,
when .... lit up the sky.

2. What terrible things did Victor Frankenstein realise?
The creature he had made was his brother's ....
He had created a ....

3. Immediately after his brother's murder, what did Victor Frankenstein feel towards the monster?
.... and ....

4. Why was the monster unhappy?
His creator didn't.................... him and wasn't.................... to him, like a father.

5. How did people react towards the monster?
They.................... and... at him.

6. What would the monster do if Frankenstein created a woman monster?
He wouldn't ....
He would learn .... and .... others.
Frankenstein .... for him.

7. What did the monster promise to do?
He promised to live where ....
to .... from people.

Part IV

1. Frankenstein destroyed the second creature because she was perhaps .... the first one.
2. By destroying the woman creature Frankenstein also destroyed the monster's .... and ....
3. The monster was left with only one feeling: .... and only one wish: ....

Part V

1. Victor Frankenstein and Elizabeth ....
2. On their wedding night, a .... broke out.
3. Victor Frankenstein was frightened by every .... and .... and decided to .... everywhere in the house.
4. But when he heard a .... and .... scream, he realised it was too late.
5. The murderer had left .... on his wife's neck.
6. The monster was watching him .... the window, with an .... on his face.
7. He .... him with his gun, but he .... and the monster ....

Part VI

1. The monster caused the death of another person, Victor Frankenstein's ....
2. The scientist is now determined to ....
3. The monster is also determined to make Victor Frankenstein feel the .... and the .... he felt.

Part VII

1. The monster felt so much pain and unhappiness in his life because
   - ☐ he knew he was doing evil but he couldn't control himself.
   - ☐ he had no family to love.
   - ☐ of both of these reasons.
2. The monster has decided to
   - ☐ destroy himself.
   - ☐ follow Victor Frankenstein to the North.
3. In the final scene the monster
   - ☐ disappears in the night.
   - ☐ is carried away by a boat.

Not dressed like that, you don't!

The diaries of a teenager... and her mother ► pages 124-127

1. General comprehension.

Who writes what?

The mother's diary is in: ☐ the blue boxes ☐ the green boxes
The daughter's diary is in: ☐ the blue boxes ☐ the green boxes

Their names	Who are they?					
Jenny	the teenager's mother	☐	the teenager	☐	a friend of hers	☐
David	the girl's father	☐	her brother	☐	a schoolmate	☐
Sadie	the girl's mother	☐	her best friend	☐	her sister	☐
Catherine	the girl's mother	☐	her sister	☐	a friend of hers	☐
Jon	a schoolmate	☐	the girl's father	☐	her brother	☐
Mike	a schoolmate	☐	the girl's father	☐	her brother	☐

2. Detailed comprehension.

15th October / 16th October

The daughter's diary.

1. What does she think about her parents?
....
2. What do her parents think about her?
....
3. Name of the exam she has to take this year: ....
4. What did her parents say about her exam?
....
5. What does she think about her exam?
....
6. What did she want to do that night?
....
7. How often does she go out?
....
8. Her parents' reaction: angry ☐ understanding ☐ indifferent ☐
9. Jenny's opinion about David:...
Why? Because he ....
....

The mother's diary.

1. Her mother's plans for that night.
2. Jenny said, " .... "
3. Her father asked, "When ....?"
4. How many times has Jenny been out this week? ....
5. Jenny's parents made her stay home. True ☐ False ☐
6. Who was:
- upset? Jenny ☐ her Mum ☐ her Dad ☐
- tired? Jenny ☐ her Mum ☐ her Dad ☐
- tense? Jenny ☐ her Mum ☐ her Dad ☐

7th November

1. Where did Jenny and Sadie go? ....
2. What did Jenny buy? ....
3. What was it like? ....
....
4. What did Sadie buy? ....
5. Back home, what did they look for? ....
6. Why didn't they use it?
....

13th December

What did Jenny look like at the school disco?	What did Jenny look like when she left her house?
clothes: .... accessories: .... any make–up?.............................. any hair gel? .... shoes: .... "look":	clothes: .... accessories: .... any make–up?.............................. any hair gel? ....

1. Jenny didn't get ready at home because she was afraid of her parents' reaction. True ☐ False ☐
2. Her mother was very angry because Jenny lied to her. True ☐ False ☐
3. Jenny was pleased because David noticed her. True ☐ False ☐
4. Jenny was late because she stayed at the disco too long. True ☐ False ☐

4th January

Jenny and her mother went to .... and visited two .... : the .... in the morning and the .... in the afternoon.

Who ...	Jenny	Jenny's mother	Both of them
would have liked to go shopping in Oxford Street?			
got bored at the National Gallery?			
found the Tate Gallery interesting?			
was interested in the young boy painting?			
was interested in culture?			
spent a long time in the gift shop?			
pretended to be interested in Monet's painting?			
doesn't like Monet's painting?			
will get an art book for her birthday?			
is going to buy a book about Monet?			
thinks the visit has been enriching?			

1st August

A Before August 1st.

1. David was Jenny's boyfriend.	True ☐	False ☐
2. Sadie was Jenny's best friend.	True ☐	False ☐
3. Jenny never talked about David with Sadie.	True ☐	False ☐
4. Sadie knew Jenny was in love with David.	True ☐	False ☐

B On August 1st.

Put the following statements in chronological order.

.... Jenny went to Sadie's house to talk to her.
.... Jenny read David's note saying he was breaking up with her.
.... Jenny didn't suspect there was anything between David and Sadie.
.... Jenny found David's note on the floor behind the front door.
.... Jenny learnt that Sadie was David's new girlfriend.

Quote from the text to show that:

1. Jenny wasn't expecting this to happen.

....

2. she is disappointed with Sadie.

....

3. she thinks that David didn't have a lot of courage.

....

4. she thinks her holiday is ruined.

....

What did Jenny decide?

☐ to get a revenge.
☐ to win David back.
☐ not to fall in love again.
☐ not to confide in people any more.
☐ to make everybody suffer during the holiday.

C Jenny's mother was "really great" because of:

1. her reaction:
☐ she asked a lot of questions
☐ she remained silent because she guessed what had happened

2. what she did:
☐ she simply listened to Jenny
☐ she complained about men

3. what she told Jenny:
☐ nobody had ever dumped her
☐ she was in love with the first boy who had dumped her

4. what she made Jenny realize:
☐ that her mother had had the same reaction as her
☐ that boys aren't important

Verbes irréguliers

Base verbale	Prétérit	Participe passé	Traduction
B			
be	was, were	been	*être*
bear [eə]	bore	born, borne	*porter, supporter* (born : *né*)
beat [iː]	beat	beaten	*battre*
become	became [eɪ]	become	*devenir*
begin	began	begun	*commencer*
bite [aɪ]	bit	bitten [ɪ]	*mordre*
bleed [iː]	bled	bled	*saigner*
blow [əʊ]	blew [uː]	blown [əʊ]	*souffler*
break [eɪ]	broke [əʊ]	broken [əʊ]	*casser*
bring	brought [ɔː]	brought [ɔː]	*apporter*
broadcast	broadcast	broadcast	*diffuser, émettre*
build [ɪ]	built [ɪ]	built [ɪ]	*construire*
burn [ɜː]	burnt [ɜː]	burnt [ɜː]	*brûler*
buy [aɪ]	bought [ɔː]	bought [ɔː]	*acheter*
C			
catch	caught [ɔː]	caught [ɔː]	*attraper*
choose [uː]	chose [əʊ]	chosen [əʊ]	*choisir*
come	came [eɪ]	come	*venir*
cost	cost	cost	*coûter*
cut	cut	cut	*couper*
D			
do	did	done	*faire*
draw [ɔː]	drew [uː]	drawn [ɔː]	*tirer, dessiner*
dream [iː]	dreamt [e]	dreamt [e]	*rêver*
drink	drank	drunk	*boire*
drive [aɪ]	drove	driven [ɪ]	*conduire*
E			
eat [ɪː]	ate [e]	eaten [ɪː]	*manger*

Base verbale	Prétérit	Participe passé	Traduction
F			
fall [ɔː]	fell	fallen [ɔː]	*tomber*
feed	fed	fed	*nourrir*
feel	felt	felt	*sentir, ressentir*
fight [aɪ]	fought [ɔː]	fought [ɔː]	*combattre, se battre*
find [aɪ]	found [aʊ]	found [aʊ]	*trouver*
fly [aɪ]	flew [uː]	flown [əʊ]	*voler (dans l'air)*
forbid	forbade [æ]	forbidden	*interdire*
forget	forgot	forgotten	*oublier*
forgive	forgave [eɪ]	forgiven	*pardonner*
freeze	froze [əʊ]	frozen [əʊ]	*geler*
G			
get	got	got	*obtenir, devenir*
give	gave [eɪ]	given	*donner*
go	went	gone [ɒ]	*aller*
grow [əʊ]	grew [uː]	grown [əʊ]	*grandir, faire pousser*
H			
hang	hung	hung	*accrocher*
have	had	had	*avoir*
hear [ɪə]	heard [ɜː]	heard [ɜː]	*entendre*
hide [aɪ]	hid	hidden [ɪ]	*(se) cacher*
hit	hit	hit	*frapper*
hold	held	held	*tenir*
hurt	hurt	hurt	*faire mal, blesser*
K			
keep	kept	kept	*garder*
know	knew [juː]	known [əʊ]	*savoir, connaître*

Base verbale	Prétérit	Participe passé	Traduction
L			
lay [eɪ]	laid [eɪ]	laid [eɪ]	*poser (à plat)*
lead [iː]	led	led	*mener*
learn [ɜː]	learnt [ɜː]	learnt [ɜː]	*apprendre*
leave [iː]	left	left	*quitter, partir*
lend	lent	lent	*prêter*
let	let	let	*laisser, permettre*
lie [aɪ]	lay [eɪ]	lain [eɪ]	*être allongé*
light [aɪ]	lit	lit	*allumer, éclairer*
lose [uː]	lost [ɒ]	lost [ɒ]	*perdre*
M			
make	made [eɪ]	made [eɪ]	*faire, fabriquer*
mean [iː]	meant [e]	meant [e]	*signifier, vouloir dire*
meet	met	met	*rencontrer*
P			
pay	paid [eɪ]	paid [eɪ]	*payer*
put	put	put	*poser, mettre*
R			
read [iː]	read [e]	read [e]	*lire*
ride [aɪ]	rode	ridden [ɪ]	*faire du cheval*
ring	rang	rung	*sonner*
rise [aɪ]	rose	risen [ɪ]	*s'élever ; se lever (soleil)*
run	ran	run	*courir*
S			
say	said [e]	said [e]	*dire*
see	saw [ɔː]	seen	*voir*
sell	sold	sold	*vendre*
send	sent	sent	*envoyer*
set	set	set	*poser, fixer, mettre*
shake [eɪ]	shook	shaken [eɪ]	*secouer*

Base verbale	Prétérit	Participe passé	Traduction
shine [aɪ]	shone [ɒ]	shone [ɒ]	*briller*
shoot [uː]	shot	shot	*tirer (arme à feu)*
show	showed	shown	*montrer*
shut	shut	shut	*fermer*
sing	sang	sung	*chanter*
sit	sat	sat	*être assis*
sleep	slept	slept	*dormir*
smell	smelt	smelt	*sentir (odeur)*
speak	spoke	spoken	*parler*
spell	spelt	spelt	*épeler*
spend	spent	spent	*passer (temps); dépenser*
spoil	spoilt	spoilt	*gâter*
spread [e]	spread [e]	spread [e]	*étaler*
stand	stood	stood	*être debout*
steal [iː]	stole [əʊ]	stolen	*voler (dérober)*
stick	stuck	stuck	*coller*
sweep	swept	swept	*balayer*
swim	swam	swum	*nager*
T			
take	took	taken	*prendre*
teach [iː]	taught [ɔː]	taught [ɔː]	*enseigner*
tear [eə]	tore [ɔː]	torn [ɔː]	*déchirer*
tell	told	told	*dire, raconter*
think	thought [ɔː]	thought [ɔː]	*penser*
throw [əʊ]	threw [uː]	thrown [əʊ]	*jeter*
U			
understand	understood	understood	*comprendre*
W			
wake (up) [eɪ]	woke (up) [əʊ]	woken (up) [əʊ]	*(se) réveiller*
wear [eə]	wore [ɔː]	worn [ɔː]	*porter (vêtement)*
win	won [ʌ]	won [ʌ]	*gagner*
write [aɪ]	wrote [əʊ]	written [ɪ]	*écrire*

Achevé d'imprimer par Grafica Veneta S.p.A. - Trebaseleghe (Pd) - Italie
Dépôt légal : 74147 - 0/13 - Juin 2012